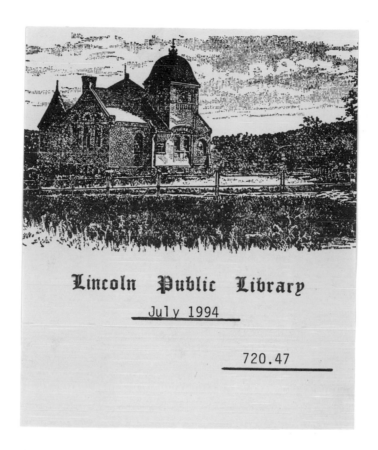

WATER AND ARCHITECTURE

WATER AND ARCHITECTURE

TEXT BY **CHARLES W. MOORE**   PHOTOGRAPHS BY **JANE LIDZ**

HARRY N. ABRAMS, INC., PUBLISHERS

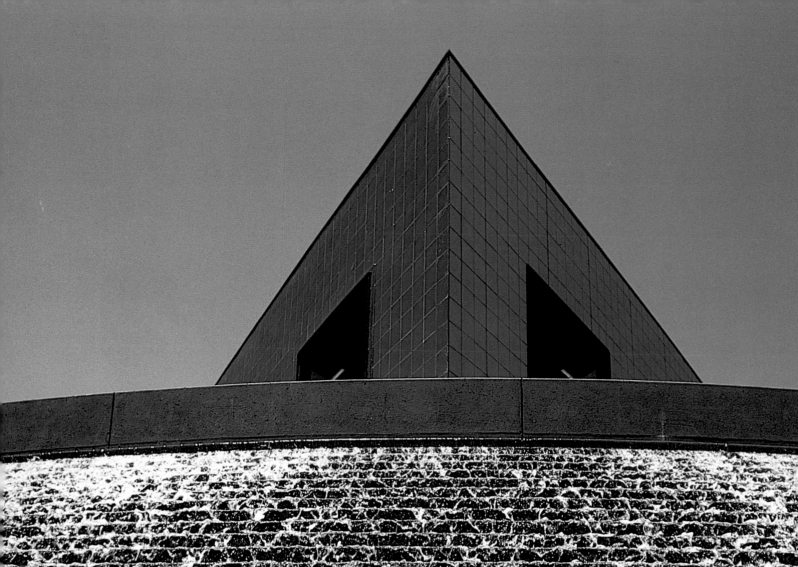

CONTENTS

Page 1: Carrasco House, Bornos, Spain.   *Page 2:* Solana, Westlake, Texas.   *Opposite:* Wateridge Marketing Pavilion, San Diego, California

WRITER'S NOTE

One of the illuminating moments of my life occurred, amazingly enough, at a piano bar on the San Francisco peninsula. In the bar, a woman was playing, splendidly, familiar Cole Porter and Steven Sondheim tunes. A man sitting at the bar began a conversation with her and, shortly afterward, extracted a clarinet from a case. It was clear they had never met, but they were soon playing together. After a while, I realized they had not played the tune of anything specific. They knew the melodies; we knew the melodies. And so their effort could go toward making beautiful figures over the familiar material—it was transporting. I then suddenly saw a future for architecture. After a half-century full of brilliant single buildings, and deteriorating towns full of macho erections that evoked the Chinese notion of yang, it was perhaps time for a half-century of yin, of healing and joining and enjoying the things we all share (like the Sondheim melodies) so that we might have a period of getting it together.

Water and architecture have always had for me a part in balancing the yin and the yang, and of restoring some semblance of balance to our teetering world. I began studying water and architecture as the subject for my doctoral dissertation at Princeton in the 1950s. Eisenhower was president, and the mood matter-of-fact. Water as architectural material was exuberantly out of step with the straight-laced times, being possessed of mysterious qualities that, for instance, relate the water in a specific place with all the rest of the water in the world. In the ensuing forty years, I have tried to absorb and learn and add to the work I began back then and finally have succeeded in bringing as much of it as possible together.

PHOTOGRAPHER'S VIEW

I t was magic. I was thirteen, standing on the banks of the river Cher in France, fascinated by the view of a castle, Chenonceaux, that had been built as a bridge. This memory was so intense that, ultimately, it became the motivation for this book.

In these photographs, my aim was to show the designer's original intent and to evoke the splendor and spirit of each place, even though some had celebrated their finest hour centuries ago. Crowds, rain, pollution, and restoration work were the reality at many of the sites. In spite of the difficulties, I was able to compose these idealized views, which have not been retouched by people or computer. Conveying the sound and motion of water in still photographs was a special challenge. Shooting a wide variety of time exposures enabled me to choose the image that best matched the babble of the brook or the crash of the waves.

This photographic journey has been a search to discover why the interaction of water and architecture is so intriguing and to capture that elusive quality on film. Recently, as I photographed Chenonceaux majestically spanning the river, I reaffirmed that this union of water and building is still an inspiration to behold.

Overleaf: Château de Chenonceaux and the river Cher, France

ACKNOWLEDGMENTS

Countless students have endured my lectures on the subject of water and architecture and have thus given me opportunities to rethink the material. Many have, through their own work, led me to new discoveries—for this I am grateful. The support of my various offices has been a tremendous boost; I am particularly grateful for the patience of my staff in the face of the frustrations of putting together such a book. I am indebted to Jane Lidz, who approached me in San Francisco with the idea of doing the book in the first place and then so enthusiastically collaborated with her wondrous photographic vision. Finally, many thanks to Kevin Keim, who worked behind the scenes to put all of this work together and lent so much energy and skill to the entire project.

C. M.

Special thanks to Bill Johnson for his help, advice, and patience in all aspects of creating this book, not least of which was being a great photo assistant and a worldwide navigator extraordinaire. Through the years and thousands of miles, his enthusiasm, muscles, and humor were constant, strong, and always appreciated.

I would also like to thank the following people for their invaluable assistance and unflagging support: my wonderful agent, Sarah Jane Freymann; the talented group at Abrams—editors Harriet Whelchel and Margaret Donovan, designer Dana Sloan, and art director Sam Antupit; my terrific office manager, Kathy Newitt; our dear friend Dee Hartman, who cared for our pets while we were away; and the best travel agent I've ever had, Christiane Rosenblatt.

For their helpful comments, I want to thank my friends and family, especially my parents, Pauline and Morris Pincus; Carolynn Abst; Mary Chomenko; Kevin Riley; Estelle Alpert; John Goldman; Paulett Taggart; Denny Miles; Lucretia Bingham; and Myra Drucker.

For their superb guidance abroad, I want to acknowledge Victor Carrasco in Spain, Wakako Murakami in Japan, Tang Benchang in China, and the many others who gave us important information and clear directions.

Finally, many thanks to Charles Moore for his inspirational ideas and continuing enthusiasm from the moment we set sail.

J. L.

Opposite: Rites of Spring Fountain, Paris, France

To Mimi, with love
C. M.

To Bill, with love
J. L.

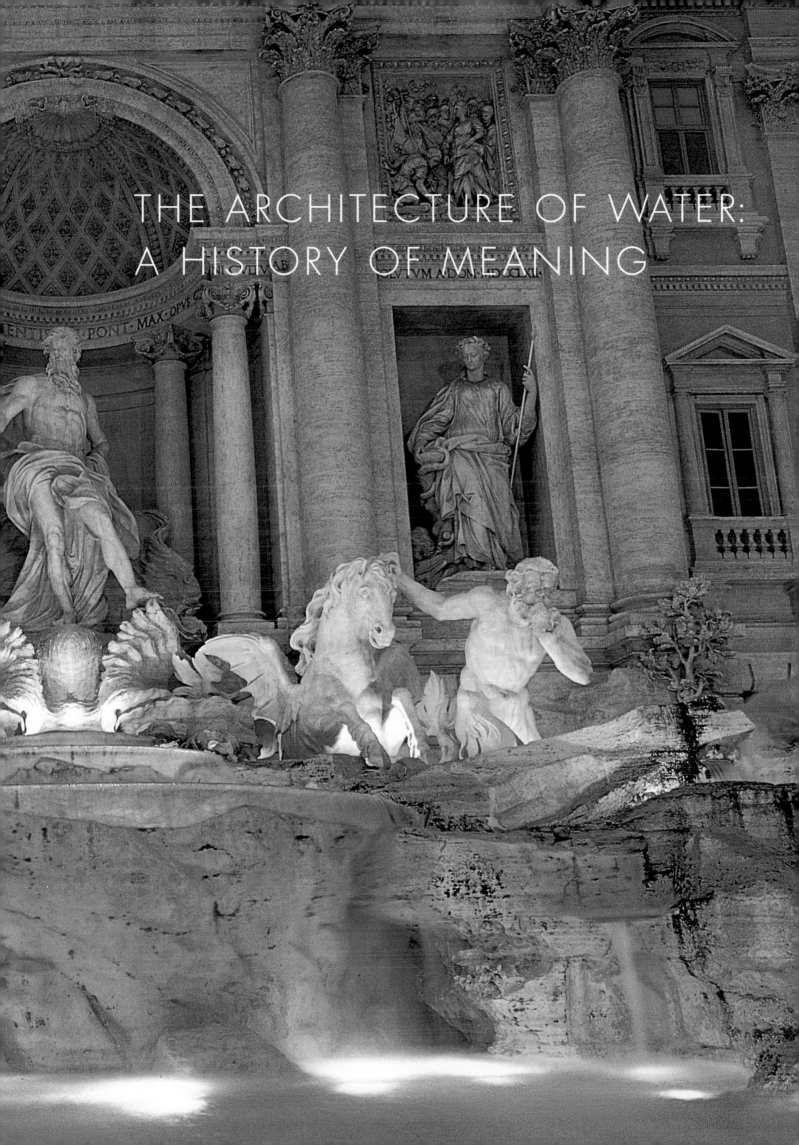

THE ARCHITECTURE OF WATER:
A HISTORY OF MEANING

Byodo-in, Kyoto, Japan

Preceding pages: Trevi Fountain, Rome, Italy

Four hundred years ago, a wise Japanese Zen master named Sen no Rikyū designed a legendary tea garden on a dramatic cliff site overlooking the Inland Sea. Despite the spectacular view over the broad expanse of murmuring ocean, the tea master carefully planted a high screen of hedges and trees all around the garden and blocked out the vista to the sea. In front of the hedge, Rikyū placed a small stone font for washing the hands, an important prelude to the tea ritual. Just above the bowl, he clipped a tiny opening through the leaves. It was a brilliantly choreographed genuflection. As visitors knelt down to the bowl, their eyes would catch a fleeting glimpse of sea through the leaves just at the moment when their hands mingled with the cool water. The tea garden was a simple but profound experience of the limited splash of water compared with the limitless ocean, the part in humbling relation to the whole, described by Sen no Rikyū as

A bit of water here,
There, between the trees—
The sea![1]

The garden has long since vanished. Today, only Rikyū's legend exists, but the lesson he leaves us is that, with only a scant amount of water and spirited design, all the water in the world can be called to mind.

Familiar and simple, yet enchantingly complex, water is endlessly appealing. We are compelled to stare at a river flowing under a bridge, to feel water as it sheets over the marble rim of a fountain, and to sit for hours transfixed by the sound of a gurgling stream or waves at the beach. From lost tea gardens to overgrown Umbrian villas to glitzy hotel-lobby fountains, we have persisted in using water in our built environments.

The key to understanding the water of architecture is to understand the *architecture of water*—what physical laws govern its behavior, how the liquid acts and reacts with our senses, and, most of all, how its symbolism relates to us as human beings. Just as the poet Muriel Rukeyser wrote that "the universe is made of stories, not of atoms,"[2] so too is water composed of stories, above and beyond its molecular fusion of hydrogen and oxygen. Whenever architects or designers include water in their compositions, they can plunge into a treasure chest of physical characteristics, legends, and allegories to enhance their designs. Our associations with water today have been shaped by our ancestors, so that the lapse of centuries adds to the symbolism, and the collected wisdom survives the tides of millennia.

The properties of water as it appears in nature are inviolable, since they are always restricted by a code of natural limits. Although its complex physical behavior cannot be completely explained by simple equations, knowledge of its properties is an important basis of design. Pure water is (or should be) odorless, tasteless, and colorless. Chemically, it is an oxide of hydrogen that covers about two-thirds of Earth's surface, with nearly two-thirds of all fresh water frozen in the polar ice caps. Atmospheric-, surface-, and groundwater are critical factors in our planet's weather systems: humidity and dew point maintain our atmosphere, ocean currents cool and warm continental temperatures, and the freeze-thaw cycle locks and releases moisture in the soil.

Water phases into a solid at 32° F (0° C) and becomes a gas at 212° F (100° C). As atmospheric pressure rises or falls, the freezing and boiling temperatures of water adjust themselves in proportion. When water freezes, it distinguishes itself from most other liquids by expanding, approximately one-eleventh of its volume; when it is a liquid, water is nearly incompressible. Two forces modify the horizontal surface of water: adhesion, or the attraction between water molecules and other materials, and cohesion, the attraction of water molecules for one another. Billions of molecules join on the surface of water to form a tension (similar to a bubble's) that always creates as small a surface as possible for a body of still water. When water moves, its dynamics are controlled by complex interactions of forces, displacements, and energies. Sprays, rapids, trickles, drops, plops, and deluges are all kinetic performances choreographed by the invisible order.

Ice, liquid, and steam are the forms of water available to designers; in these three conditions, the water may move within itself, lie still, flow, steam, freeze in icicles, billow up in fog, fall down, spout up, or flake. Liquid is used most often, but solid ice and vaporous steam must also be confronted, since architecture is a part of the environment where they are commonly present. In fact, a pictorial catalogue of water phenomena would require most of the world's scenery to be complete. Thin, silent glazes of undisturbed northern lakes reflect the heavens like hand mirrors for the gods. Forest streams glide through dense Appalachian undergrowth. Plunging cascades in Venezuelan rain-forest waterfalls fill the atmosphere with mist, drowning the humid air with thundering silence. Fog banks arriving from the sea barely clear Irish coastal cliffs, then move inland to roll over hills and valleys like phantoms. Rains fall in a soothing drone and transform Tuscan cities of stone into watercolored mirages of pastel wetness. In Japan, water sweats up from thermal volcanic arteries collecting in steaming baths inches away from crystalline mounds of snow and ice. Even though chemistry and physics dictate the action of water everywhere in the world, the vast range of qualities that water is shaped into by the environment sets the stage for profound poetic interpretation and inspiration for architects.

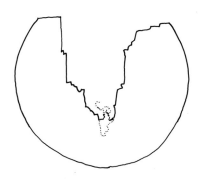

In water lurk the mysteries of time. "There is a kind of river of things," Marcus Aurelius wrote in his *Meditations*, "passing into being, and Time is a violent torrent. For no sooner is each seen, then it has been carried away, and another is being carried by, and that, too, will be carried away."[3] Ripples in ponds expand from the plunk of a stone endlessly outward, while the gravitational tugs of the moon hypnotically seduce ocean tides in and out. Rivers snake through deep canyons painstakingly carved out by their waters eons before. Rapids surge ahead, as unflinching as chronological time, while the canyon walls that echo the white water's crash are layered with a geological code of what once was. Drenching monsoons arrive to mark seasonal transitions and their natural rhythms year after year. Far beyond the penetration of light, ocean depths seem to be places sequestered from time, where eerie pressurized worlds are inhabited by our evolutionary ancestors. Up above, the ocean horizon traces the line of infinity, while waves roll in, endlessly doling out the passing years, decades, and centuries. Fountains, with their marble lips smoothed by the water's persistent polish, gurgle alone late at night, patiently giving lessons in transience.

The metaphors of water are rich to the point of paradox. Along with earth, air, and

Annibale Carracci
Landscape with the Flight into Egypt. c. 1603
Oil on canvas, 48¼ × 98½"
(122.6 × 250.2 cm)
Galleria Doria Pamphili, Rome

fire, water had long been regarded as one of the four basic elements of the universe. Under the medieval law of interdiction, it was forbidden to supply banished criminals with fire or water, since both were essential for survival. More than anything else water is a source of life and the great symbol for life. All life depends on water; nothing escapes its influence, and nothing lives without it. This life-giving water appears over and over as a common thread woven through the religion, literature, and art of every culture. "Everyone who drinks of this water will be thirsty again," Saint John wrote in his Gospel. "The water that I will give will become in them a spring of water gushing up to eternal life."[4] Many centuries before Christ, Lao-tzu, the father of Taoism, wrote: "The supreme good is like water, which nourishes all things without trying to. It is content with the low places that people disdain. Thus it is like the Tao."[5] In the Koran, water is a gift from God, a token to mortals of divine omnipotence and omniscience: "Have not those who disbelieve seen how Heaven and Earth were once one solid mass which We ripped apart? We have made every living thing out of water. Will they still not believe?"[6]

In China, where earth has commonly been viewed as a living organism, water cherished as a manifestation of the Tao pointed to the path of natural order. Chinese watercolorists often included water in their landscapes as a sign of life, either collecting in pools or flowing through rivers or waterfalls. "Water is a living thing," noted Kuo-hsi in his *Essay on Landscape Painting*, "hence its aspect may be deep and serene, gentle and smooth; it may be vast and ocean-like, winding and circling. It may be oily and shining, may spout like a fountain, shooting and splashing; it may come from a place rich in springs and may flow afar. It may form waterfalls rising up against the sky or dashing down to the deep earth; it may delight the fishermen, making the trees and grass joyful; it may be charming in the company of mist and clouds or gleam radiantly, reflecting the sunlight in the valley. Such are the living aspects of water."[7] Water as a sign of life appears in Western art as well. It is not a coincidence that, in his *Landscape with the Flight into Egypt*, Annibale Carracci places the water source in the center of the lunette, at its compositional focus. Water is the central source of the ideal landscape's life-giving heart.

Despite water's role as a common denominator for life, it has also been seen as a symbol of death. As complex and vital as it can be, it can also be empty, dark, and cold. Until modern times, water, mysteriously aloof within its arterial network of subterranean passages, was feared as an evil force. Water relentlessly dissolves bonds, it spoils, it drowns, it wears away, it rots, and it floods. It even unravels memory. "Here lies One Whose Name was writ in Water"[8] was the epitaph twenty-five year-old John Keats suggested for his own tombstone in Rome's English Cemetery. Water consumes fire, and heat consumes water, but on their own, they are equally threatening.

> *Water and fire shall rot*
> *The marred foundations we forgot,*
> *Of sanctuary and choir.*
> *This is the death of water and fire.*[9]

warns T. S. Eliot in the *Four Quartets.*

Leonardo da Vinci studied the motion of water obsessively. After watching rivers rise above their banks and swallow up defenseless countryside and towns, he was convinced of the menacing side of water. "Among irremediable and destructive terrors," he wrote in his notebooks, "the inundations caused by rivers in flood should certainly be set before every other dreadful and terrifying movement, nor is it, as some have thought, surpassed by destruction by fire."[10] Far from repressing his terror, Leonardo made it his frequent concern. His charcoal drawings of floods and tempests are patterns of passionate swirls. Dark and foreboding, evoking the fears that rushing waters elicit, they are paradoxically seductive in their uncontrolled play.

Tame water, particularly when it is reflective, fresh, and clear, suggests youthful health and beauty. From ancient Bath to modern Saratoga Springs, people have flocked to spas to bathe in therapeutic pools. Drinking special waters also has been linked to good health: ancient Greece had springs where only the immortal gods were privileged to imbibe, and today the craze sustains a booming market for extravagantly plain bottled water. The ultimate spring is the mythic fountain of youth, whose charmed waters magically wash away birthdays and somehow smooth out the wrinkles of time. Juan Ponce de León's legendary quest for the fountain in Florida and the Caribbean in the early six-

Leonardo da Vinci
Drawing from *The Deluge* series. c. 1517
Black chalk and brown and yellow inks
6⅜ × 8" (16.2 × 20.3 cm)
Windsor Castle, Royal Library
© Her Majesty Queen Elizabeth II

Sandro Botticelli
The Birth of Venus. After 1482
Tempera on canvas, 5'9" × 9'2"
(175.3 × 271.8 cm)
Galleria degli Uffizi, Florence

teenth century was only a tall tale (his chief pursuit was for gold), but his exploits inspired imaginative stories of expeditions for the precious water. In Frederik Paludan-Müller's nineteenth-century novel *The Fountain of Youth*, the Spanish knight Diego de Herrera (standing in for Ponce de León) discovers the magical waters on the island of Bimini: "He sprang up hastily from his couch and advanced to the pool. There his youthful form, which he very well remembered, like that of a youth of twenty—with beaming look, dark eyebrows, fresh colour, and curly locks—was visible; and, full of life, advanced to meet him from the mirror of the wave below."[11] Conversely, stagnant water can besmirch the promise of youth and point to the inevitable decay of body and mind— William Blake warned to "expect poison from the standing water."[12] Moreover, the absence of fresh water betrays a thirst for youth and the unavoidable loss of innocence and vitality. Shakespeare's "liquid dew of youth"[13] rarely outlives the morning, and with the heat of the afternoon, old age creeps in, as Eliot wrote, "Here I am, an old man in a dry month, / Being read to by a boy, waiting for rain."[14]

Abundant water is a symbol of fertility. People "waiting for rain" around the world have devised all kinds of rituals to cajole rainmaking gods. In the *Golden Bough*, the English scholar Sir James Frazer described several rituals that emphasized the connection between water and the fertility of the earth.[15] In Halmahera, Indonesia, the ritual leader would shake a dripping bough at the soil to encourage the clouds to open up. Rain-charmers in New Britain would bury a wet bundle in the ground and then imitate the plashing of water with their mouths. The Omaha of North America would fill a large vessel with water, dance around it, sip the water, and squirt it into the air. Then they would empty the vessel onto the ground, the dancers would fall to the earth, lap up the spilled water, and squirt it back out again. Sometimes the fertility of women would be called upon as an added inducement. In India, naked women and girls hoping to charm rain from the sky would go out in the middle of night and pull a plow through the fields. Water as a symbol of fertility is also a popular metaphor of seduction and contact. Rather than deriving fertility from the earth, Aphrodite inherited her seductive power from the sea, out of which she had risen in her Botticellian scallop-shell debut. D. H. Lawrence repeatedly alludes to steamy desire in *Women in Love* by emphasizing wetness and moistness: "After a lapse of stillness, after the rivers of strange dark fluid richness had passed over her, flooding, carrying away her mind and flooding down her spine and down her knees, past her feet, a strange flood, sweeping away everything and leaving her an essential new being, she was left quite free, she was free in complete ease, her complete self."[16]

When water is pure and clear, it can also indicate chastity. According to legend, a virgin sprite named Trivia led a band of parched Roman soldiers in 19 B.C. to the source of a secret spring near Salone, a town east of Rome. For the local townspeople, such an underground spring was the stuff of folklore—no one had ever actually seen or tasted the water, but it was endowed with magical, restorative powers. When the soldiers took news of the discovery back to the city, Marcus Vipsanius Agrippa, the master builder of Augustan Rome, ordered the construction of an aqueduct to carry the water through the *campagna* to the city. This unusually pure and sweet-tasting liquid became known as the Aqua Virgo, Latin for virgin water—according to the hydrologist Sextus Julius Frontinus, "It was called Virgo, because a young girl pointed out certain springs to some soldiers hunting for water, and when they followed these up and dug, they found a copious supply."[17] The legend of the dancing maiden spread quickly, as did the water she led the soldiers to. In a survey of the Roman waterworks, Frontinus tabulates that by A.D. 70 the Aqua Virgo was connected to 2,504 taps in Rome, distributing the clear, pure water to basins, camps, public buildings, and ornamental fountains.

Linked to water's role as a symbol of chastity is its power as a cleansing agent. Physical purification that leads to spiritual rejuvenation is a recurrent water metaphor. In the Christian tradition, water signals the introduction into spiritual life and the promise of eternal salvation. Not only does it wash the body in the Old Testament, but it also cleanses the soul: "I will sprinkle clean water upon you, and you shall be clean from all your uncleanesses, and from all your idols I will cleanse you."[18] In the New Testament, a baptismal plunge in the river Jordan would purify the soul by washing away sins. At the height of religious festivals in India, thousands flock to the Ganges for ritual immersion. Despite the fact that the river is usually brown and muddy, its purifying, redemptive power is never diminished. The water points to something beyond itself; it acts as a bridge, spanning the gap from physical reality to symbolic surreality. "*E*mersion," the Romanian-born theorist Mircea Eliade emphasizes in *The Sacred and Profane*, "repeats the cosmogonic act of formal manifestation; *im*mersion is equivalent to a dissolution of forms. This is why the symbolism of the waters implies both death and rebirth. Contact with water always brings a regeneration—on the one hand because dissolution is followed by a new birth, on the other because immersion fertilizes and multiplies the potential of life."[19] Water makes a tangible connection: it can be felt cooling the skin and surrounding the body. But it is also invested with an intangible presence, made evident by its undulant nature: as it flows, surrounds, and swirls, it remains ungraspable and uncontainable.

Central to every one of these symbols, prominent in high-school science texts and the army manual of water supply, is the water cycle. With the help of gravity and evaporation, the cycle circulates water around the planet, guaranteeing that every drop of water in the world—whether in rushing streams, icebergs, water spilt on the kitchen floor, underground lakes, cups of tea, tears, or the limitless oceans—takes part in the process. The ways that architecture and water relate can be divided among the four general stages of the water cycle—fountains, rivers, pools, and oceans.

The water cycle was long misunderstood. A legion of philosophers and scientists strained their wits for centuries to explain its mysteries. Thales, Plato, Aristotle, Isidore, and many in between speculated about such perplexing problems as the origin of springs, the destination of rivers, the source of rain, and the oceanic edge of the flat world. Almost all of them compounded the mysteries by inventing mythical subterranean realms rigged with tangles of intricate plumbing systems or celestial waterworks controlled by trapdoors and stratospheric reservoirs.

Even though many water mysteries were solved over time, the origin of springs—where fresh water came from, how it got there in the first place, and where it went after disappearing into the ground—stubbornly persisted as the missing link in a unified water-cycle theory. In 1580, after centuries of conjecture, a French potter, author, and scientist named Bernard Palissy pieced together a plausible explanation for this phenomenon, but it was not until 1723 that his theory was widely disseminated. In that year, the Paduan scientist Giovanni Poleni presented a paper to the Royal Society of London in which he clearly outlined the process responsible for the return of water, borrowing both from Palissy's earlier work and from hydrologic theory developed over the centuries. First, Poleni concluded, fresh water emanates from one of two sources: either below ground in the form of springs or above ground as streams. Then the water naturally flows downhill and collects in lakes or ponds or flows into rivers. Eventually, the rivers run into one of the oceans and mix with their salty waters. From the surface of every lake, river, puddle, and ocean, water evaporates into the atmosphere, where it condenses into clouds or fog. Gusty winds push and pull the clouds around the atmosphere until the right conditions allow the molecules to condense and fall back to the earth as rain, sleet, or snow, to be absorbed into the terranean system, where the process can begin again.

Fountains symbolize both the emergence and disappearance of fresh water. When water bubbles up naturally from a spring, it speaks of the origin, the beginning, or the source of life. At the other end of the cycle, as water seeps into the earth, it evokes the cyclical return and journey back to the source, with images of departure, death, and hoped-for return. For all of history, people depended on fresh water, so its source was always an important place—where people gathered, settlements flourished, and cities were established. Within towns or cities, then, fountains typically designate important urban places. Even today, when most cities do not rely on public fountains for their water supplies, fountains still become focal points in communities.

After emerging from springs, water travels downhill through natural streams or man made canals until it reaches a level container or flows into a larger river. Running streams of water can range in size from gargantuan—flooding rivers hundreds or thousands of miles in length—to tiny brooks nestled in forest glens. Rivers were important tools for developing societies; they helped trade to expand and prosper, sustained agriculture with irrigation, and supplied hydropower for mills and factories. Industrious societies used canals to link seas and oceans interrupted by the continental landmasses, to extend rivers, to pull the ocean inland, to connect lakes, rivers, and bays, and even to substitute for city streets. With their directional motion, canals and rivers are waters of communication and connection, linking cities and empires, or, on a smaller scale, figuratively networking gardens or courts with miniature canals too narrow or shallow to navigate.

Streams, rivers, rains, and springs fill lakes and pools, where water rests before it evaporates into the atmosphere or drains to lower elevations. Lakes embody notions of collection and reflection; their glassy surfaces and calm bodies contrast with the energized liquid of fountains and rivers. Lakes and ponds have thus always been an important ingredient in the Romantic landscape gardener's recipe, forming a horizontal sheen within gardens that pacify the psyche and become repositories of dreams. Like rivers, lakes also have a synthetic alternative—the pool.

The sea, with its brute force and overwhelming reach, has had the most power to challenge society and stifle our efforts, just as its immeasurable scope has also stirred our emotions and dreams. The sea's fundamental metaphor is the eternal, evoked by its vast volumes and broad horizons. When cities or buildings are built near oceans, both the realities and the poetics of continental edges must be addressed. At the sea's edge, designs can make use of the mythic as well as the actual continuity of water to develop a suggestion of distant, almost infinite space. But designs can also evoke a sense of immediacy and contact so that spectators feel intimately connected to the ocean. The nature of such edges varies; the meeting point of land and water may be a gradual sandy beach with rolling dunes, a rocky shore, a sheer cliff with a jagged promontory, a sheltering harbor, or a built-up city. When we build on those bits of land surrounded by water, which we call islands, a profound poetry of isolation and separation can be attained, especially when finite islands are engulfed by infinite seas.

Any study of architecture and water has at its disposal a rich history of meaning and tradition as well as a foundation in mesmerizing physical and natural wonders. When the fusion of architecture and water is treated carefully and creatively, the potential for meaningful expression is practically limitless. The world of water embraces every culture; each has its own way of designing with water and including it in architecture. Epics of water and architecture stretch from misty Suzhou to the verdant Amazon. Japanese gardens, Texas parks, and English landscapes rely on water, as do Hong Kong skyscrapers, Venetian neighborhoods, and French châteaus. It is in Rome, however, that a true understanding of the phenomenal odyssey of water and architecture must begin.

From the Via di S. Vincenzo, an old Roman street, a distant echo of moving water floats over the crowded buildings and reverberates through the narrow urban canyon. At the end of the street, off to the right, Corinthian columns flank the entrance to the church of SS. Vincenzo e Anastasio, whose facade noses into a piazza. Across the piazza, a palazzo mysteriously erodes away. First, a twisted crack splits its travertine pilaster, then rocks crumble from its face, and, finally, large boulders tumble off into a pile of rubble, magically fusing with natural rocks down below. As one enters the piazza, the sound of gushing water steadily mounts to a gentle rumble, then suddenly the street bursts into the sunlight and a crash of water engulfs the senses. Out in the open, water rushes everywhere. The Trevi Fountain rises into full view, commanding attention as it overcomes the piazza with its formidable delight. Here, water makes its jubilant entry into the city.

Architect Nicola Salvi envisioned the fountain (completed in 1762) as a glorious affirmation of the water cycle—something of a celebration of compatriot Giovanni Poleni's contributions to water-cycle theory. "The Sea is, so to speak," Salvi wrote, "the perpetual source which has the power to diffuse various parts of itself, symbolized by the Tritons and the sea Nymphs, who go forth to give necessary sustenance to living matter for the productivity and conservation of new forms of life, and this we can see. But after this function has been served, these parts return in a perpetual cycle to take on new spirit and a new strength from the whole, that is to say from the sea itself."[20]

Michelangelo Buonarotti
The Creation of Man. 1511
Ceiling fresco
Sistine Chapel, Vatican, Rome

At the Trevi's helm, Oceanus towers in the center of a triumphal arch. As the mythic protector of the sea and a godfather to the Greek pantheon, Oceanus guards the wellspring of life and commands its torrential release. With an outstretched arm, he rushes unreservedly into the wind, which ruffles his beard and flaps his cloak into a frenzy of marbleized drapery. Beckoning to a pair of winged stallions with his index finger, he charges them with life, just as Michelangelo's Sistine Chapel God of Creation does for Adam. These horses symbolize the arrival of fresh water, straight from its underground source. One stallion, representing tame and placid waters, is obedient, but the other steed, which refers to violent, uncontrollable deluges, rambunctiously struggles against the taut reins. Sheets of fresh water cascade around this aquatic menagerie, denoting the distribution of fresh water everywhere in the world. The water collects in the enormous basin that signifies the ocean and, simultaneously, more water squirts back up into the air, symbolizing the completed cycle. All around, water splashes, foams, churns, spits, caresses stone reefs, and, at night, its luminous sparkles dance on the facades of neighboring stone walls, windows, and medieval arcades.

The Trevi is the ultimate joining of water and architecture. Like the water it plays with, the fountain is a repository for countless dreams and fantasies. Yet despite its mythic and grandiose theatricalities, the Trevi never loses its amazing ability to relate to everyday customs. People gather daily around the fountain to bask in the sun and spray and gossip about politics, the price of vegetables, and the latest neighborhood scandal. In the evening, the Trevi is a mandatory stop for locals on the *passeggiatta* circuit, while droves of tourists ritually flip a small fortune of lire, quarters, or marks over their shoulders into the basin, supposedly guaranteeing them one special wish as well as a return trip to the Eternal City.

Overlooking all the activity is a stone panel most of the time unnoticed by the Trevi's visitors. This carved relief, above Oceanus's left shoulder, depicts a young girl standing to the side of a group of men who observe a spring gushing from the ground. The water of the Trevi, then, in constant agitation down below the panel, is the same water that the virgin sprite Trivia led the soldiers to on that hot summer day two thousand years before. Having already outlived one language, the Italian Acqua Vergine continues to stream from the same ducts as the Latin Aqua Virgo so long ago. It is the water of Frontinus and Augustus, ebbing and flowing, rising and falling at the side of the many empires it served. Gesturing to the present by looking back to the past, the fountain links the symbolic with the physical. With a relatively small amount of water, all of the world's water is called to mind, and it is water that provides the lifeblood for meaning in architecture.

Above and opposite: Trevi Fountain, Rome, Italy

Overleaf: Venice, Italy

Lighthouse, San Giorgio, Venice, Italy

Opposite: Solana Marriott, Westlake, Texas

Overleaf: Saiho-ji, Kyoto, Japan

Villa Lante, Bagnaia, Italy

Opposite: Bank of China, Hong Kong

Fort Worth Water Gardens, Texas

Ryoan-ji, Kyoto, Japan

FOUNTAINS: WELLSPRINGS OF THE MYTHIC WATERS

B. B. Andreini
The Garden of Eden. From L'Adamo, *sacra representatione*, Milan. 1617

mages of Eden are well known. Visions abound of a lush biblical paradise teeming with life, saturated with extraordinary beauty, devoid of sin and sorrow, and probably free from traditional garden enemies as well—no hungry rabbits, toxic pesticides, or fruit flies. All species live together in harmony under perpetual sunrises: wolves sleep with lambs, lions roam with deer, humans and mosquitoes live in peace. In the heart of paradise, where this pleasing life first came into being, a fountain quietly gurgles, fed from a spring issuing from a divine, otherworldly source. As described in Genesis, the water "flows out of Eden to water the garden, and from there it divides and becomes four branches."[21] Splitting into the Pison, Gihon, Tigris, and Euphrates rivers, the wellspring of Eden distributes the water beyond the garden walls. Clearly, the fountain represents the wellspring of life—magical waters with immortal connections.

Throughout history, fountains have symbolized sacred sources, the origin of life, and the initial stage of the water cycle. Metaphors for life and sustenance are common in poetic fountain imagery. Henry Wadsworth Longfellow describes the heart as a fountain of affection:

> *Talk not of wasted affection, affection*
> *never was wasted;*
> *If it enrich not the heart of another, its*
> *waters, returning*
> *Back to their springs, like the rain, shall*
> *fill them full of refreshment;*
> *That which the fountain sends forth*
> *returns again to the fountain.*[22]

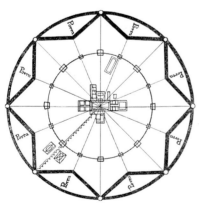

Antonio Averlino il Filarete
Ideal City of Sforzinda. From *Codex Magliabecchianus*, Florence. c. 1457–64

Preceding pages:
Fort Worth Water Gardens, Texas

Just as blood returns to the heart in a life-sustaining cycle, water circulates through the global cycle to nourish the earth, ultimately returning to its fountain heart-source to be renewed. A good illustration of this is a fifteenth-century plan by Il Filarete for an ideal city called Sforzinda (so named for his Milanese patrons), which features a fountain strategically positioned in the center of the concentric composition. "In order to limit noisy wagon traffic," Filarete explained, "and to provide greater convenience for the inhabitants, we will surround the Piazza and other markets with navigable canals and make every other principal street a porticoed water street–canal. . . . A great reservoir will be placed in the Piazza [the highest point in the city] from which an overflow will flood and wash all the streets and squares."[23] Not only does the fountain distribute water for Sforzinda's imaginary inhabitants, but the water source affirms that the piazza is the center of the city, and the outward flow establishes visual and symbolic connections with the outlying parts of the plan.

Four stone river gods perching on a travertine mountain in the center of Rome symbolize the notion of a central wellspring and water's global distribution. Out of a Baroque convolution of marble gods, travertine seaweed, and stone dolphins spews Acqua Vergine, piped in from the Trevi Fountain. The water travels under Domitian's Circus Agonalis (site of ancient gladiatorial contests) and emerges under an Egyptian obelisk in the center of the modern Piazza Navona, now enclosed by dwellings, shops, palaces, and churches. The obelisk's enormous weight seems to plug the geyser that percolates underneath, forcing the water to squeeze out from under the pavement through every fissure in the rock. Coursing water lifts the river gods' bare feet in the air, rocking them with its powerful rhythm. The four colossal figures—representing the Nile, the Ganges, the Danube, and the Río de la Plata—symbolize the unified world of Genesis updated according to seventeenth-century cartography. Each god is adorned with native accoutrements to identify his continent: an armadillo sniffs around the New World de la Plata with its stash of coins, a boa constrictor slithers around the Ganges, a Pamphili coat of arms shields the Danube, and the veil draping the Nile's face represents its then-unknown source, not identified until 1858, when the English explorer John Hanning Speke came upon the vast headwaters.

The Fountain of the Four Rivers was designed and built between 1647 and 1651 by Gianlorenzo Bernini, who relished the spirit and energy of a world suddenly turned inside out. Both fountain and architect became flamboyant centerpieces of Roman art and society. Bernini kept company with popes and princes who celebrated his prodigious talents as a sculptor, architect, painter, poet, and socialite in courts across Europe. For Romans, the fountain's obelisk pinpointed their city as the center of the rapidly expanding world, resulting from the century's groundswell of discovery and learning—the age of Copernican revolution. Only decades before, in 1609, Galileo Galilei had constructed the first complete astronomical telescope, opening a window into the unfathomable depths of the universe. Isaac Newton would soon follow with his laws of universal gravitation and calculus, revolutionizing physics and mathematics. And European conquistadors were brutally colonizing the Americas while explorers were continuing to map Africa and Asia.

The Fountain of the Four Rivers was also once the center of the pageantry of Baroque theater. Romans loved to seal the neighborhood drains on seventeenth-century Sunday mornings and fill the piazza with water like a colossal bathtub. Instead of chariots roaring around curves Ben Hur–style, boats and waterlogged carriages would make their way

Giovanni Paolo Pannini
Piazza Navona Allegrata. 1756
Oil on canvas, 37⅞ × 53⅝"
(95.5 × 136 cm)
Niedersächsisches Landesmuseum,
Landesgalerie, Hannover

through the "Lago Navona" carrying members of the loftier circles of Roman society. The aristocratic Pamphili family (who furnished the Holy See with Pope Innocent X in 1644) presided over the festivals from their palace on the edge of the piazza, which the pope and his domineering sister, Olimpia, lavishly embellished as a showcase for their family's influence and power. Legend has it that when Innocent stubbornly resisted bankrolling an expensive fountain in the square, Olimpia and Bernini, plotting in tandem, placed an exquisite silver model of it in his bedroom, firing the pope's imagination with the brilliant design.

One enters the piazza from one of the narrow side streets to see the distant blur of the spiny mountain rising in the center. As one gets closer and closer to the fountain, its astonishing detail comes into focus. The fluvial gods, carved from silken Carrara marble, contrast with the rocks and plants, which are hewn from grainy, porous travertine. The fountain provides endless fascination in the play of its water against the stone. Where water runs, Bernini polished the travertine smooth, but the areas it does not he left rough and coarse so that the solid stone seems to dissolve over time. "Nothing in the world," Lao-tzu wrote, "is as soft and yielding as water. Yet for dissolving the hard and inflexible, nothing can surpass it."[24] Over the years, the flowing water has deposited minerals in streaks and patinas, leaving rich shadows and gleaming highlights. At night, underwater lights dapple on the stone, creating the illusion that the figures are actually moving: the river gods swinging their legs in the air, the stallion struggling, and the dolphins' flippers splashing in the water. From the slender stone shaft, to the flip of a dolphin's tail, to the gods' uplifting energy, the fountain moves the eye heavenward, releasing one's mind to the sky. Against the upward lift, and following a rhythm of its own, water spills from the mound, falls into the stone bowl, and drains down into the cave, always, inevitably returning to the dark source.

Explaining the source of water was a difficult hurdle in understanding the water cycle. Prior to the discoveries of Bernard Palissy and Giovanni Poleni, many pondered the enigma. Thales of Miletus believed that water was the most fundamental building block of the universe—irreducible and indestructible—but could not explain where it ultimately came from. No outright physical phenomenon accounted for the riddle of the water cycle's origin, so the ancients assumed that an alien mechanism hidden beneath the earth's surface had to be responsible for its uncanny movement. (A contemporary illustration of this theory is Isamu Noguchi's fountain in Costa Mesa, California, where the water flows through a strange landscape and vanishes into a secret portal carved in a mountain.) But what force propelled water back into the sky or to the mountaintops, where precipitation and springs always begin their downward rush? In *Phaedo,* Plato wrote of subterranean worlds where "enormous everflowing underground rivers and enormous hot and cold springs, and a great deal of fire, and huge rivers of fire, and many rivers also of wet mud" led to a chasm "bored right through the earth."[25] The netherworld reservoir fed Oceanus, the great river that encircled the earth, wrapping the horizon with its uninterrupted flow. To keep the water in motion, Plato theorized that a seesaw perpetually rocked back and forth, sending the vast tidal pools of water rushing to and fro. Beyond the unknown (which for the ancients meant essentially everything past the Pillars of Hercules) was the fearful nothingness, where, without warning, the ocean would suddenly career over the edge of the flat plate.

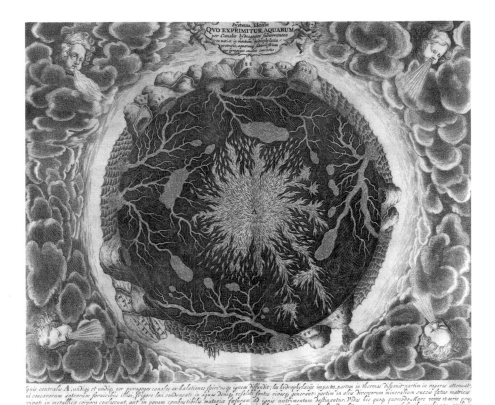

Athanasius Kircher
Mundus Subterraneus. 1678
Engraving, 16⅛ × 14⅝" (41 × 37 cm)
The Beinecke Rare Book and Manuscript
Library, Yale University

Aristotle debunked Plato's notions, charging that his "description of rivers and the sea in the *Phaedo* is impossible. . . . For if they flow towards the centre and also away from it, they will flow uphill as much as down, according to the direction in which the surge of Tartarus inclines. And if this is so we have the proverbial impossibility of rivers flowing uphill."[26] In the thirteenth century, Thomas Aquinas also rejected the seesaw theory, professing a more saintly view that the sea rises to the summit of mountains because the water is attracted by heavenly stars. Engravings from Athanasius Kircher's *Mundus Subterraneus* of 1664 depicted the center of the earth as a molten core in which pools of boiling liquid forced water through arteries up into mountain interiors, where springs emerged and fed the rivers that flowed back down to the sea.[27] Isidore, the seventh-century bishop of Seville, who was an avid naturalist and scientist, had been equally convinced of the idea of an abyss. "The abyss," he wrote, "is the deep water which cannot be penetrated; whether caverns of unknown waters from which springs and rivers flow; or the waters that pass secretly beneath, whence it is called abyss. For all waters or torrents return by secret channels to the abyss which is their source."[28]

The abyss is a potent fountain metaphor even in the twentieth century. In Fort Worth, Texas, water rushes wildly into Philip Johnson's artificial umber canyon, pours through channels notched into the stone, and spills into a pool. The gargantuan drain is a watery black hole, a grand spectacle dramatizing the hydrologic vanishing act. At the rim of the gulch, water emerges; streams of feathery water slide unabated down the inclined walls, gather in a river (Oceanus) that rings the pit, and constantly feed torrents of smaller gushers that are in turn swallowed by the gaping mouth. In the pool, the foam churns and froths like a boiling cauldron. One suspects that it is bottomless. The steps along the inner walls of the gorge are without protective railings or barriers so that visitors make their way gingerly to the bottom, while water slicks only inches beneath their feet, amid an engulfing thunder of cascading water. It is a liminal world of both danger and delight. Where the water goes after it is sucked into the pool remains in the realm of imagination.

Fountain water can be inspiring (Four Rivers) or threatening (Fort Worth Water Gardens), but it can also be life-giving and purifying. From an ancient Typikon of Jerusalem, a chant is sung on Good Friday:

> *And Thy life-giving side, like a fountain bubbling forth from Eden,*
> *Waters thy Church, O Christ, like a reasonable Paradise,*
> *Thence dividing into sources, into Four Gospels,*
> *Watering the universe, purifying creation,*
> *And teaching the nations faithfully to worship Thy Kingdom.*[29]

The combination of fertility of the "life-giving side" and the notion of "purifying creation" reinforces two important images of the water source. Before the advent of modern plumbing, fountains and their networks of aqueducts and cisterns were essential systems in towns or cities. To emphasize their importance, people since ancient times have decorated their civic wells and fountains with symbols of their town's history or the mythology associated with the water source. For instance, in Siena's main square, or *campo*, a series of she-wolves fill the Fountain of Joy. The basin is surrounded by an assortment of statues and reliefs that connect notions of liquid flowing from the "life-giving side" with biblical and mythological tales (Romulus and Remus, for instance), thereby identifying water as a literal and mythological life-source of the city.

Although modern showers and baths also have replaced the ancient system of public bathing, fountains and baths can still evoke notions of cleansing and the "purifying creation." Roman bathhouses were monumental buildings lavished with monumental budgets; in Japan natural baths bubbled up from volcanic arteries; and, in Saratogoa Springs, New York, each fancy bathhouse was given its own architectural style. England's only hot springs spew 250,000 gallons a day into pools in Bath, an ancient Roman city built around the bathing tradition. Long ago, the Romans had converted the existing baths, dedicated to the Celtic god Sulis, to an establishment in homage to Minerva. Modern excavations have uncovered very elaborate and sophisticated chambers that featured three different

Bernard Forest de Belidor
Garden engraving, from *Architecture Hydraulique*. 1737–53
The Harry Ransom Center, The University of Texas at Austin

types of baths for different water temperatures—the chilly frigidarium, the lukewarm tepidarium, and the steaming caldarium. In the twelfth century, local monks built newer baths over the Roman ones, most notably the King's Bath, which for the next several centuries was the favored bathing spot (supposedly with curative waters) for the aristocratic families of England.

Bathing, of course, was not limited to ancient Roman or medieval English traditions. In Sebatu, Bali, ebullient quintets of fountains spill into a series of deep bathing pits that are surrounded by lush and fertile palm canopies. On the ledge above each basin, a council of stone deities meditate as sacred waters flow below their knees. The five fountains keep the water in constant motion. Bathers descend into the pit between high stone walls that sink directly into the water, reinforcing their removal from the world at large and connecting them more intimately with the water source and nature.

The key to making successful and captivating fountains is to control the way water moves to produce whatever effect is desired (animating, enlivening, relaxing, soothing, exploding, dancing, swirling, or splashing) without losing control of the water or ruining the fountain with tangles of pipes, wires, or gizmos. Nature provides the best models. Water moves through the environment in an endless variety of ways: it rushes turbulently in brooks, falls in drops or mists or sheets of rain, rises from springs in trickles, or bubbles up into pools. Water thunders over falls, rolls onto beaches in waves, crashes against rocks, flurries in blizzards, and condenses in drops of dew.

Even when water is not available, one can create a sense of nature's flow and fall with other materials. Sculptural curves can allude to water, or geometrically patterned tile can substitute for water seasonally drained from fountains. Many Japanese gardens incorporate dry cascades of pebbles and stones that act as stand-ins for absent water. Dehydrated streams and cascades at the Daisen-in or the gardens of Saiho-ji in Kyoto are made with small, white pebbles raked to resemble currents of water that swirl around rocks and stumps and pass under small bridges made with slabs of stone.

Fountains can also assert mastery over nature, with stilled water controlled in a geometric shape or spouting water jetted against gravity by machinery. While most Oriental gardeners abstained from shooting and spraying water, seventeenth- and eighteenth-century French architects and landscapers very consciously tried to *forcer la nature*, enthusiastically assembling water devices to produce dazzling effects, some natural and some mechanical. These designers were not, however, trying to stifle or upstage the nature that they were forcing. Instead, they sought to animate and enrich nature by applying the reason and technology they had developed. Water spouting through nozzles was admirably suited to help achieve these ends, since designers could easily alter and improvise upon the nozzles' shapes and sizes. Salomon de Caus catalogued the technical principles of fountain design in the *New and Rare Inventions of Water Works*, published in 1659. De Caus clarified specifics of fountain design, including laws of water displacement, plumbing systems, mechanical motors, and principles of fluid dynamics.[30] Bernard Forest de Belidor followed with *Architecture Hydraulique*—published in four volumes between 1737 and 1753—an extraordinary encyclopedia of water and architecture. Lighthouses, naval war machines, port scoopers, water mills, pumps, and hydraulic organs were only a few of the topics he explained and lavishly illustrated. In his last chapter, "De la Décoration des Jardins," De Belidor suggested ways architects could use moving water

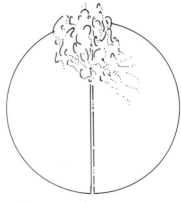

Jet d'eau

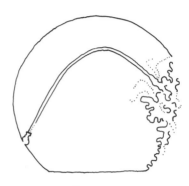

Berceau

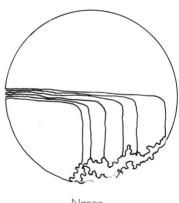

Nappe

Cascade (waterfall)

in the gardens of château clients. An advocate of jetting water, De Belidor listed the following principal water shapes: *jets d'eau, berceaux, nappes, cascades, grottes, bassins, gerbes, arbres d'eau, grilles, champignons, buffets, fontaines,* and *théâtres.*[31] Many of the fountain forms were derived from nature and are standard shapes still used today.

Jets d'eau shoot up vertically from the ground, forcing water out of its natural horizontal plane. They appear in nature as geysers, like the postcard one at Yellowstone National Park, whose water is sprayed into the air with a regularity that endlessly delights summer tourists. Machine-made jets can be towers of water similar to the one in Lake Geneva (the world's tallest, 575 feet high, is in Arizona), or they can be midget jets that bubble up in pencil-thin squirts, as in the Alhambra in Granada, Spain. Jets can be solitary plumes breaking the horizon or a plane of water, or several can be arranged in a line, grid, or pattern to make them seem more numerous and multiply their delight. Jets d'eau can dignify a place with their stately, fluid, vertical axes, or create impressive allées like the ones lining the entrance canal to Peterhof near Saint Petersburg. They can also be whimsical and frolicsome: at Fountain Place in downtown Dallas, Dan Kiley, Peter Kerr Walker, and WET Design collaborated on a water extravaganza featuring more than two hundred jets that send water into the air in cadences programmed by computers in a kind of visual music. The jets may appear as short plumes that bubble out of the holes, shyly venturing out a little farther in up-and-down rhythms, until finally they blast into ectomorphic flagpoles of water. The water sometimes erupts without warning and soaks anyone standing above the holes, coming up through sockets that are flush with the pavement so that obtrusive pipes do not trip frolicking hydrophiles. After the water reaches its peak, it falls back over the jet in white suds and slinks back into the hole.

When jets d'eau are tilted out of plumb, the resulting parabolic shapes are called *berceaux,* whose streams have trajectories manipulable by increasing or decreasing the water pressure and direction. Powerful berceaux with four-inch calibers can be shot by water artillery, such as the blasting cannons near the base of the Eiffel Tower. Gentler arcs are more appropriate to the small courtyards of the Generalife in Granada, Spain. There, in the south pavilion, two rows of slender berceaux crisscross in midair over a long rectangular pool to form a perspective of water loops and cool the hot Spanish afternoons. Similar berceaux in other parts of the garden have metal workings that swivel so that gardeners can change the direction of the streams and water the groves of myrtles, orange trees, and cypresses.

Like jets, berceaux can have less formal applications. At the Epcot Center in Orlando, Florida, Peter Fuller and Allen Robinson (later founders of WET Enterprises) designed berceaux that are like comets without their tails. Circular pods arranged in two rows send blobs of water leaping through the air (like Mexican jumping beans); children try to catch them as they zigzag across and down the sidewalks, each magically landing back in a pod. Niki de Saint-Phalle and Jean Tinguely's collaborative fountain in Paris is a plumbing system gone berserk and a delicious counterpoint to the watertight plumbing encapsulating the adjacent Centre Pompidou. Tinguely's contraptions and motors gyrate Saint-Phalle's brightly painted figures, flinging splashy berceaux around in revolving squirts and lashes.

When water flows in thin sheets over smooth ledges, the streams are called *nappes.* A nappe can free-fall over an edge (as its English equivalent, "tablecloth," suggests) or can slide over a weir, or dam, in a smooth, rounded glaze. People are fascinated with water that is trained into the thinnest possible sheet. They love to feel the edge with their fingers and break the perfect stream with their hands. Ricardo Legorreta's fountain at the Solana development in Westlake/Southlake, Texas, has an extraordinary nappe that is squeezed into a thin tongue of water by a square channel. Bold violet and ocher stucco walls contrast with and highlight the purity of the water that falls through the air in a stream. Louis Kahn's reflecting pool at the Kimbell Art Museum in Fort Worth is split-level: a shimmering plane of water slips in a smooth plume over the edge of the container into a wider pool below. In Bath, England, the river is regulated by a triple weir that creates a broad water amphitheater, spreading under Robert Adam's eighteenth-century Pulteney Bridge.

Cascade (plume)

Cascades imitate splashy waterfalls. Their surfaces are not smooth and glassy like nappes but are broken up into fractured streams, white foam, and wild squirts. The ultimate cascade is at Niagara, where millions of gallons of water dangerously career over the broad American and Canadian falls, once a symbol of courage for those willing to ride in a barrel over the edge. At the Lovejoy Plaza in Portland, Lawrence Halprin and I designed a cascade in a water park. We made steep concrete walls notched out with steps and seats that channel a white-water stream excitingly close to visitors, playing against the steps and ledges as if they were natural rocks and boulders. Water cascades over the walls to stacks of twisted steps in imitation of a Sierra cascade, with white water, cool mist, and velvety noises to appease city dwellers. Also noteworthy is the cascade at the Mirage resort in Las Vegas: a relatively ordinary waterfall by day, at night it is magically and mysteriously set aflame.

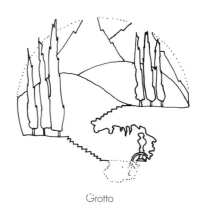

Grotto

Grottes (or grottoes) are caves that contain mythical water sources. They are traditionally built underground with stone vaults to synthesize moss-covered caverns, sometimes inhabited by earthy water gods, nymphs, or goblins who trickle water from their mouths or breasts. De Belidor recommended *rocailles, congelations, pétrifications,* and *coquillages* (rocks, coagulations or stalagmites, petrified things, and shells) to achieve the desired *rustique* effect of being underground, damp, dark, and cool. During the Renaissance and up until the seventeenth century, grottoes were fashionable in Italian, French, German, and English gardens. Bernard Palissy designed a grotto for Catherine de' Medici on the royal grounds of the Tuileries in Paris, there is an enormous and creepy grotto in the Florentine Boboli Gardens, and Papa Giulio had an elegant "nymphaeum" built in his Roman villa, guarded by four caryatids.

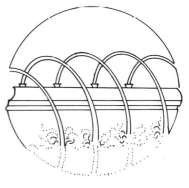

Basin

Bassins (or basins) are pools that collect and contain the water from jets, nappes, or cascades. They are sized to harmonize with the available space and positioned carefully to take advantage of their reflective surfaces. Basins find their natural equivalents in lakes and ponds. At French gardens such as Versailles or Vaux-le-Vicomte, architects built enormous basins to distinguish important visual axes and create formal patterns of glazed water that mirror the sky and moving clouds overhead. Sometimes they positioned fountains in the pools so that the stilled water would make a dramatic, splashing escape and send rippled shock waves across the surface. These basins are normally flush with the ground, interrupted only by their container's thin borders. When basins are lifted out of the ground, water that spills over their lips becomes expressive features of the fountains: smooth edges permit the water to flow unbroken, ridges and moldings break the water into drops and splashes.

The wonder of fountains is that they are limitlessly variable: all of De Belidor's basic shapes can be mixed and improvised on to generate new fountain forms as illustrated in one of his imaginary water gardens. For instance, a *gerbe* is made by bunching several

Grilles

small jets in a basin to form a pyramid of water. When air is pumped in, the noise of thunder and rain is created. *Arbres d'eau* are tree forms with branches and leaves of water. A stately fleur-de-lis in Rome's Piazza Farnese sends out a shower of liquid diamonds sparkling in the morning light. *Grilles* consist of many little jets lined up in a row below a landing. *Champignons* of water are thick low jets sprouting in the shapes of mushrooms. *Buffets* and *fontaines* include a marble table, statues, and vases that release all kinds of water shapes, making a *montagne d'eau* of multitiered water displays.

Each fountain form has its appropriate place, but sometimes they can all be combined into a grand composition known as a *théâtre d'eau*. At the Grand Wailea Resort in Maui, the designers pick and choose from well-known precedents and translate them into tropical scenes of palm trees, tiki huts, and jungle waterfalls. Here one finds the Alhambra's south pavilion with its berceaux laid out between green lawns and swaying palm trees, Monet's water pond glimmering over a giant mosaic water lily, the pools of Versailles lined with palm trees, stretching toward the beach and lifting perpendicular jets against the horizon—all of the variations strangely wonderful and wonderfully strange.

A fountain does not have to be grand, though, or require exotic flushes of water to be successful. Spirited design can substitute for extroverted deluges. Within the old Roman ghetto, the Tartarughe (Turtle) Fountain quietly inhabits the thoroughly ordinary Piazza Mattei. At one time fountains were usually at the ends of aqueducts, where the water pressure was the mightiest and the need for distribution most urgent. The Tartarughe, however, is a long way from its own aqueduct and its corresponding water pressure. Challenged by the absence of dramatic water, the anonymous designer created a charming fountain that is a lazy counterpoint to the exuberance of most Roman fountains.

The water is contained above in a shallow basin filled by a weak jet. Limp berceaux squirt in thin streams through the air and land in a larger basin below. Four boys surrounding the pedestal nudge a quadruplet of turtles toward the coveted dish of water. Below, thicker spurts pass through the mouths of fish and mix with the rest of the water. Since the weak pressure ruled out any uplifting surges or loud cascades, the upward motion of the youths stretching up to just touch the struggling tortoises with their fingertips substitutes for the absent dance of water in the air and alludes to its cyclical return to the source. Water brings the eye downward, but the sculptural movement helps to move the spirit back up again.

Fountains are hypnotic; as psychological outlets they are enduringly charming. Not only does the refreshing play of water attract people, but water and its stories are a source of constant fascination for landlocked city dwellers. The Barcaccia Fountain in Rome (allegedly designed by Gianlorenzo Bernini's father, Pietro) alludes to a fleet of boats sunk long ago in a mock naval battle staged in Lake Nemi. Its design was inspired by excavation of the rotten skeletons of the ancient ships. The "bad barge" now rests at the base of the Spanish Steps in Rome, where water floods the leaky hull, slowly sinking the boat below the pavement. The tub is low and flat with graceful upturned ends and sensual, curvilinear forms whose openings allow the water to spill over. Carved sun faces spew scalloped plumes of water (fashioned by flat, crescent-shaped nozzles) that play against the stone curves around them. There is something wonderfully useless about a water-logged barge, especially one that obfuscates the mad rush of Fiats around its base. Even with the ever-increasing traffic, the Barcaccia stubbornly remains, still remarkably able to block out the chaos above, in what Richard Wilbur once described as the "fountain-quieted square."[32]

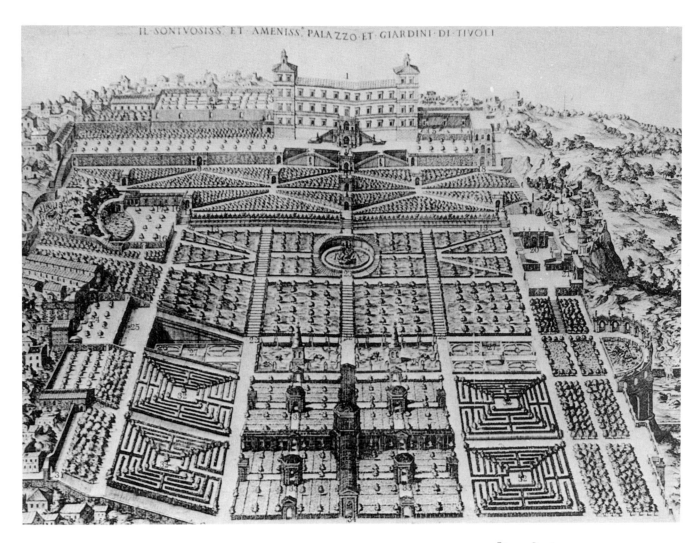

IL SONTVOSISS. ET AMENISS. PALAZZO ET GIARDINI DI TIVOLI

Etienne Dupérac.
The Villa d'Este at Tivoli. 1549
Engraving

Fountains that take exhausted minds back to nature find their greatest expression in the magnificent Villa d'Este, the most spectacular théâtre d'eau in the world. Spread out on a steep slope in the Latium Hills, the garden contains innumerable variations of foun tains and the forms imaginative designers can give water. The land where the gardens and water came to life was deeded in 1550 to Ippolito II, Cardinal d'Este, a man of leg endary tastes, who required that his gardens be the most extravagant, ornate, and fanci ful in Europe, ultimately inspiring countless gardens around the world. Principally designed by Pirro Ligorio, the gardens in their glory had a stunning array of elaborately orchestrated fountains.

Ligorio linked hundreds of fountains in a series of liquid episodes—gurgling or flow ing, gushing or seeping, springing or churning—following one unifying theme: the water source. A reservoir above the villa collects water from the river flowing through Tivoli. Each morning, around 11:00 A.M., after enough water has been amassed, gardeners open the valves, releasing water down the hillside and stirring the grounds to life. Water from one fountain spills over its carved concave lip, rushes down the slope, disappears beneath the garden steps, and passes through a staircase railing to activate another fountain down below. Every fountain relies on another for its water. If one fountain is plugged with leaves or fingers, then the next one in the sequence coughs and sputters. Hidden in the trailing ivy, leprous stone faces drool into streams flowing past, merging with more water dripping from another monster down the line. The most glorious expression of this liquid continuity is the Avenue of the One Hundred Fountains. Lining a long terrace, nozzles direct water upward. The water fans out in the chlorophyllous garden light and then falls back to the stones in drops, forming rivulets among the moss and plants. In between, berceaux leapfrog down the line past vigilant D'Este eagles, while the row of one hundred jets squirt in succession, forming the famous water perspective.

The garden was not meant to be entered from the top (where visitors today are required to enter) but at the bottom gate, where a tall cypress nave along the central axis frames the view of the distant hilltop villa. Just inside the lower entrance, a small trickling fountain provides an introduction, while an earth goddess in a nearby grotto extends her arms and distributes water from her many breasts to the thirsty, fertile gardens. Moving up the hill, transept sidewalks extend from the main axis while the fountains steadily get bigger, wetter, and louder. Shaded paths lead to a stone arcade with a room made entirely by a veil of showers. Water gushes from massive pillars to fill an oval basin that receives invading, long-range berceaux. Nearby, crashing cascades are flung back up in the air by a firing range of jets d'eau, enlivening an elaborate stage setting for concerts at the hydraulic organ up above. In another fountain, water replaces fire in a stone dragon's toothy mouth while urns marching up the balustrades shoot arcs of water at the imaginary flames. Across the garden, in the opposite wing, a miniature city, once a scaled-down model of Rome, surrounds a sunken barge. Over the years, jets, cascades, and sprays have saturated the stone metropolis, disintegrating the magnificent buildings into crumbly shells. Throughout the garden, the soft curves of the walks and balustrades blend with the natural contours and slopes. Erupting jets d'eau imitate in white water the similarly shaped green cypresses in the distance. While water is immediate and close enough to be felt, it can also be viewed in the distance, springing, dancing, and rushing through *la bella natura*. Finally, in the courtyard of the villa, at the top of the hill, a fountain with one small jet ends the performance that began down the hill with the equally tiny fountain at the gate.

The lesson of the Villa d'Este is that water is a natural material, and that, although controlled by gravity and natural laws, it can be coaxed, shaped, and transformed. We can try to achieve harmony with nature, we can try to ignore it, or we can try to master it—or we can find ourselves, at the end of the twentieth century, in a confused, ecological attempt to do all three at once. As we in our century have steadily removed ourselves from the ideals of nature celebrated by the Villa d'Este, we have risked losing intimate contact with water. This is depressingly obvious in our modern urban environments. At the Bank of China in Hong Kong, I. M. Pei's fountain is an essay on dual personalities as it transplants a morsel of nature into a city where steel-and-glass skyscrapers dominate. On one side of the fountain, a romanticized spring comes up from the pavement, with rocks, streams, and miniature cascades recollective of delicate Chinese gardens. On the other side, the natural materials mutate into hard, geometric forms. Irregular stones become triangular slabs, the slope is carved into a series of corrugated steps, and the rush of water regulated into a uniform and constrained flow. In the hard, unforgiving landscape, the sounds of water on rocks take tired minds back to nature, relieving, for a moment, the claustrophobia and hectic pace. Yet the mechanical side also reminds of the debilitating consequence of banishing nature from our cities.

Away from the madding cities, in the tranquil Ryoan-ji gardens of Kyoto (a sort of Japanese Eden, where water is for the garden what electricity is for a modern city—its lifeblood), the water source is recalled in a simple fountain, pieced together with bamboo and string, nestled unobtrusively in the rocks and plants. Water streams through the hollow bamboo shafts, empties into a small pool, and spills between the moss and pebbles. Through its very simplicity, the fountain dignifies the water, makes it special, respects and cherishes it. The water has the amazing ability to represent realities above and beyond itself, calling to mind something altogether larger.

Water, in all of its variations, interpretations, and presentations, shares a simple, common origin. It has inherent, immutable properties that time cannot alter. This fountain, like the infinitely more complex and grand Trevi or Four Rivers fountains, celebrates exactly the same idea, that, with enough care, even a few drops of water can represent the poetic splendor of the water source. In the words of Nicola Salvi, the architect of the Trevi Fountain, fountains and the water they give forth "can be called the only everlasting source of continuous being."[33]

Ritual baths, Sebatu, Bali

Villa d'Este, Tivoli, Italy

Villa d'Este, Tivoli, Italy

Opposite: Farnese Fountain, Rome, Italy

Saint Francis Woods, San Francisco, California

Tartarughe Fountain, Rome, Italy

Overleaf: Plaza de España, Seville, Spain

Fountain of the Four Rivers, Rome, Italy

Opposite: Il Moro Fountain, Rome, Italy

Barcaccia Fountain, Rome, Italy

Fountain of Joy, Siena, Italy

Overleaf: Villa d'Este, Tivoli, Italy

L'Esposizione Universale di Roma, Rome, Italy

Generalife, Granada, Spain

Overleaf, left: Hyatt Regency, Scottsdale, Arizona

Overleaf, right: HemisFair Park, San Antonio, Texas

Fountain Place, Dallas, Texas

Prometheus, Rockefeller Center, New York

Opposite: Rites of Spring Fountain, Paris, France

Fort Worth Water Gardens, Texas

RIVERS OF CONNECTION, CANALS OF COMMUNICATION

ater begins its descent into the terraced gardens of the Villa Lante in Bagnaia, Italy, from a grotto at the top of the hill. Beginning with overgrown green canopies on the highest level, each garden terrace becomes increasingly elaborate and spacious, culminating in a carefully manicured parterre on the lowest level. The water also becomes increasingly tamed as it descends: first, the water oozes from the grotto and then is sent down the hill until it reaches the pools at the bottom. In its flight, the water sluices down the central axis, passing underground from fountain to fountain, occasionally emerging to glide through a series of granite vertebrae or splash down flights of stairs. The channels tap into showers, discreetly disguised in building details, that drench unsuspecting visitors; they fill pools where river gods recline lazily and spurt through champignon fountains in pencil-thin water jets. Midway through the garden, the canal resurfaces to glide the length of an outdoor dining table (placed on axis), forming a trough for chilling wine. Monsters with mossy complexions lurking beneath the table act as conduits for the continuous stream just before it vanishes beneath the garden once again. For its final appearance, the water mists from the Gambera family crest on the last terrace (over-

Preceding pages:
Precious Belt Bridge, Suzhou, China

Villa Lante. 1600s
Engraving

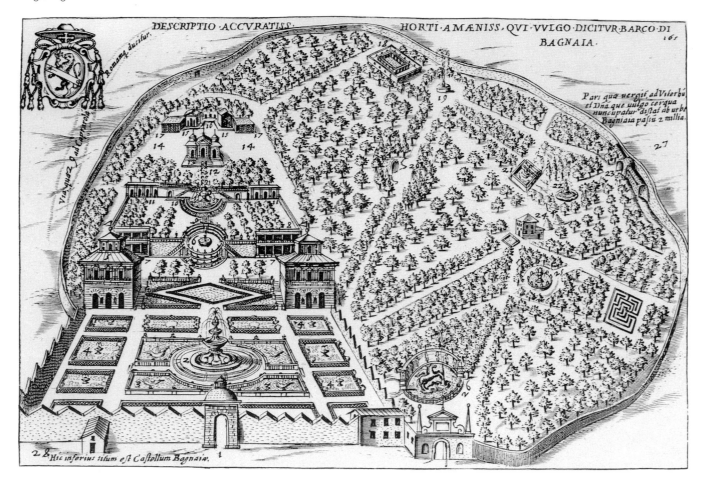

76

looking the roof clusters of Bagnaia) and finally falls obediently into the parterre pools.

Giacomo da Vignola, it is believed, planned the villa in 1566 for Giovanni Cardinal Gambera. Vignola's idea was to combine fountains (source) and canals (distribution) as a liquid framework for the villa and its gardens. Like the Villa d'Este, the Villa Lante's gardens are arranged on a sloped site, with terraces carved into the hill and fountains punctuating the course to the sides of the main axis. But at the Villa Lante, the water dominates the axis of the composition. The villa's twin casinos are placed off to the side in a surprising deviation from conventional villa design, in which the main building is the central, dominant part of the composition. Just as Leon Battista Alberti instructed in *De re aedificatoria* that "bright streams of water must run through the garden, and above all must start up unexpectedly, their source a grotto,"[34] the Villa Lante's grotto releases the water and canals send it rushing down the garden's central axis, which forms the villa's spinal column. The continuous stream of water establishes a core; through it we understand the garden as a *whole*, a harmonious body, and a complete thought.

If fountains are the wellspring, or the heart-source, of water, then canals and rivers, in extension of the metaphor, are the arteries and veins. "I've known rivers," Langston Hughes wrote, "I've known rivers ancient as the world and older than the flow of human blood in human veins. / My soul has grown deep like the rivers."[35] Like veins and arteries, rivers and canals are waters of connection and communication. The word *fluency* refers to mastery of a language—words flow from the mouth in a comprehensible stream—which affords communication. The flow of sentences or rivers (*flumen, fiume, fleuve, Fluß*) establishes a continuum, so that in communication they link ideas and expressions, and in connection they link places or time. Canals can be symbolic connectors and communicators too. In Panama, for instance, the famous canal provides not only a physical link between the Atlantic and the Pacific but also a symbolic corridor between East and West, summed up by its slogan, "the land divided, the world united."

Rivers are classic examples of water arteries that flow not only through space but also through time. Although their positions remain essentially the same, rivers are kinetic elements—the flowing water constantly renews itself. "You could not step twice into the same river," Heraclitus noted, "for other waters are ever flowing onto you."[36] On ink-wash scrolls, Chinese artists depict rivers as an element of space connecting the hazy emerald Yangtze hills of the background with the foreground of hills, rocks, and fields. The Chinese word for this connecting void (filled with energy) is *ch'i*, the same word used by acupuncturists as they look for the energized connections in the human body, thought of in art as *lung-mo,* or "dragon's veins."

João Gilberto's Brazilian songs, on the other hand, chronicle in bossa-nova rhythm the objects or emotions that a river encounters as it flows through the landscape, endlessly changing, endlessly flowing. Edgar Allan Poe's "The Domain of Arnheim" also evokes a river's journey through space and time. Poe describes a vast ideal landscape, carefully designed in all its parts, with water as the central artery that focuses the composition. As Poe's imaginary river threads its way toward the mythical city of Arnheim, it becomes the medium through which the landscape is revealed. From "shores of a tranquil and domestic beauty," the river flows between "impenetrable walls of foliage" and through a gorge where the "crystal water welled up against the clean granite."[37]

"I have left to the last the dynamic component of the city," Lewis Mumford wrote,

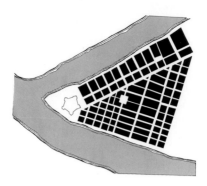

Pittsburgh, Pennsylvania

"without which it could not have continued to increase in size and scope and productivity: this is the first efficient means of mass transport, the waterway. That the first growth of cities should have taken place in river valleys is no accident; and the rise of the city is contemporaneous with improvements in navigation, from the floating bundle of rushes or logs to the boat powered by oars and sails."[38] The Tigris, Euphrates, and Nile are among a few rivers that have earned legendary status, not simply for their size and power, but because their waters link our present with the ancient cities and cultures that originated on their banks.

According to an early Sumerian epic, the creation of the Tigris and Euphrates coincided with the birth of the universe.

> *Now that the "fate" of the universe has been decreed,*
> *Dyke and canal have been given proper direction,*
> *The banks of the Tigris and Euphrates have been established,*
> *What else shall we do?*
> *What else shall we create?*[39]

In response to this quandary, there arose some of the earliest known civilizations, where writing, agriculture, and government first appeared. Ur, Nippur, Babylon, Uruk, and Sumer germinated in the flat plain—the "fertile crescent"—between the two rivers. Mesopotamian hands filled the cradle with mountainous ziggurats and hanging gardens (kept green by irrigation channels extending from the twin rivers), the first recorded wells and canals, and the ill-fated tower of Babel. Everything relied on the nutritive flow of water.

The Nile and its water permeate everything Egyptian, from creation myths of men and women springing from the tears of Ra, to colossal temples with column forests capped with bundled river reeds, to hieroglyphic river symbols carved in pyramid tombs guiding travelers to the afterlife. Like a giant water ribbon, the Nile connected all Egyptian cities, pyramids, villages, temples, and towns into one entity, a civilization. In fact, the Nile defined Egyptian citizenship. "Egypt," according to the Greek historian Herodotus, "is all the land that the Nile waters in its course and that they are Egyptians who, living lower than the city of Elephantine, drink from the water of the Nile."[40] The Roman architect Marcus Vitruvius Pollio wrote about the importance of water for the Egyptians, whose lives depended on the yearly flooding of the Nile valley: "Hence also those who fill priesthoods of the Egyptian tradition show that all things arise from the principle of water. Therefore, after carrying water in a vessel to the precincts and temple with pure reverence, they fall upon the ground, raise their hands to heaven and return thanks to the divine goodwill for its invention."[41] Every year, the overflowing river replenished the topsoil in thin strips along each bank (beyond its reach was the sandy void of lifeless Saharan dunes), which changed the layout of the land and erased property lines and borders, limiting the civilization's eastward or westward expansion.

The Mississippi is a river deeply American. A nationwide network of feeders (the Saint Croix and the Kaskaskia from the east and the Skunk and the Arkansas from the west, for example) drain into the Mississippi as it surges to the Gulf of Mexico. Linking northerly Saint Cloud, Minnesota, with southerly New Orleans, Louisiana, the river's unrelenting volume seems to energize America's pioneer spirit. Many writers examining this spirit and its people came to the river for answers. One cannot imagine the Mississippi without Mark Twain; his tales and characters have as much to do with the river as its

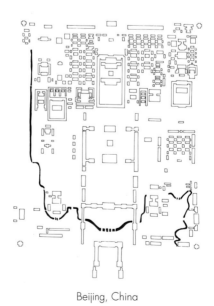

Beijing, China

riverboats, levees, docks, Deep South towns, or plantation houses. In *Life on the Mississippi*, Twain exhorts: "It was with indescribable emotions that I first felt myself afloat upon its waters. How often in my school-boy dreams, and in my waking visions afterwards, had my imagination pictured to itself the lordly stream, rolling with tumultuous current through the boundless region to which it has given its name, and gathering into itself, in its course to the ocean, the tributary waters of almost every latitude in the temperate zone! I looked upon it with that reverence with which every one must regard a great feature of external nature."[42] T. S. Eliot, who also grew up near the Mississippi's banks, never forgot the river's symbolic power:

> *I do not know much about gods; but I think that the river*
> *Is a strong brown god—sullen, untamed and intractable,*
> *Patient to some degree, at first recognised as a frontier;*
> *Useful, untrustworthy, as a conveyor of commerce;*
> *Then only a problem confronting the builder of bridges.*
> *The problem once solved, the brown god is almost forgotten*
> *By the dwellers in cities—ever, however, implacable.* [43]

Manhattan, New York City

Through the accumulation of myths and history, rivers have come to evoke not just places, but places in particular times: the Rhine of a Wagnerian opera, the icy Delaware of Washington's heroic crossing, the Thames of King George II's courtly regatta, or more grimly, the Conemaugh, site of the Johnstown flood of 1889.

Ever since people have built cities along rivers, the configuration and flow of the streams have generated the layouts for streets, avenues, and parks. The patterns of river-city compositions are limitless. Pittsburgh, Pennsylvania, is indelibly connected not to one river but three: the city rises from the triangular plot of land created by the Alleghe ny and Monongahela as they converge to form the Ohio. Grids parallel to each river extend into the city and become the streets and blocks. In the center of the city, the grids come together at an angle, resulting in superimposed city blocks and views. In contrast, Beijing's snakelike river establishes a winding counterpoint to the formal, gridlike arrangement of orthogonal palaces and courts of the Imperial Palace. Rivers can divide metropolitan regions in half, as the Mississippi does when it flows between Minneapolis and Saint Paul, or the Danube as it waltzes through Budapest. Manhattan is a series of grids squeezed between the East and Hudson rivers; the same is true of Philadelphia, between the Delaware and the Schuylkill. Charleston, South Carolina, lies at the junction of two rivers, the Cooper and the Ashley. Proud residents have deemed their city the place where "the Ashley and the Coopah meet to form the Atlantic!"

A major factor in river cities is the way the city forms an edge to the water. The combination of land and water is always charged with potential drama since the transition between them can be abrupt and riddled with psychological contrasts. In some cases, the city may keep the river at bay. Walls may elevate the street level above the river's surface, dams may alter or block its flow into the city, or barriers may prevent pedestrians from getting close to the waterway's edge. Rome is locked in the elbow of the Tiber (its "forgotten brown God"), whose opaque sludge indicates the Roman street level of antiquity; the modern streets are now elevated forty feet above. Boston, Massachusetts, and Austin, Texas, have not neglected their river gods but have developed parks along the Charles and the Colorado so that bicyclists and joggers can escape city traffic and exercise along

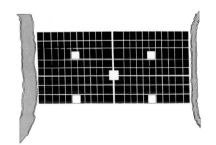

Philadelphia, Pennsylvania

Rome, Italy

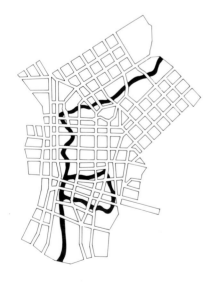

San Antonio, Texas

the scenic paths up and down the banks. Lower Slaughter in the English Cotswolds has a narrow river passing through the village that comes very close to houses, with bits of open space and trees along its course. Not only does the river physically connect the land-locked town with outlying parts of England, but it also psychologically connects the villagers with the distant sea. London has more formal and regal edges with its river. The Thames is lined with handsome Georgian buildings, the Houses of Parliament, and a myriad of bridges and towers, all leading to the mouth and port.

San Antonio, Texas, is very near the source of its namesake river. As the river cuts through the city, a loop breaks off near the Alamo, passes under a series of bridges, and reconnects with the straight path eight hundred yards farther along. Earlier in this century, the river had been twenty feet below the level of the city, useless for commerce and a menace during floods. After a flood in 1921, local businessmen decided to connect the straight parts and fill in the loop, whereupon the ladies of San Antonio "rose up like Trojan wives and got the plan vetoed."[44] They permitted the bypass to be excavated but insisted that the loop be preserved and made into a "River Walk." What they saved was a city inexorably bonded with its river. The River Walk's banks are bordered with shops, inns, cafés, cantinas, and an outdoor theater where the audience and stage straddle the river. A sidewalk linked by small footbridges alternates along opposite sides of the waterway.

The River Walk has the amazing ability to isolate people from the rest of the city. Walls block out the city's noise, the water cools the air, and live oak branches cantilevering over the river filter the intense Texas sunlight. Most important is that only a few railings stand between the sidewalks and the river. The only barrier, a small curb (as one would find on any street), indicates the boundary between pavement and liquid and strengthens the connection between the people and the water. This river, so fearlessly included in the design of the city, gives the city its center—not a heart, but a central artery full of intimate connections. People come together along the fluid Main Street and are coaxed by the liquid diplomat to a kind of public life and interaction reminiscent of an American civic tradition regretfully close to extinction.

Paris is also a premier river city that has not lost its intimate connection with its waterway, so full of connections both intangible and tangible. Artists have tried for generations to capture the constantly changing and elaborate courtship between Paris and the Seine. Claude Monet's water chameleon rolls under the hazy blur of the Pont Neuf, mimicking the atmosphere's unpredictable moods and colors. It travels through the city and through time, somewhere along the way transforming into singular dots that blend into Georges Seurat's mirages of utopian river-park life. The river, whose tree-lined banks can be glimpsed through openings in the Tuileries, down a crowded avenue, or from a roof garden poking through cracks in the skyline, establishes a reference point for the viewer. It makes one feel a part of the city and individually connected to its geography and its history.

As the Seine makes its way through the city within its walled and sunken channel, its course is punctuated by monuments, squares, parks, and landmarks. The river links the Place de la Bastille, the prow of the Île de la Cité splitting the river in half (carrying its Gothic cargo and tugging the Île-Saint-Louis), the Louvre, the Madeleine, the Hôtel des Invalides, and the thrust of the Eiffel Tower at the other end of the city. Like Heraclitus's river, today's Seine is and is not the same river that cleansed the blood from the Place de la Concorde during the Revolution, or hailed the *moderne* of the 1889 Exposition Universelle, or inspired Gertrude Stein's "lost generation" on the Left Bank. Along the ser-

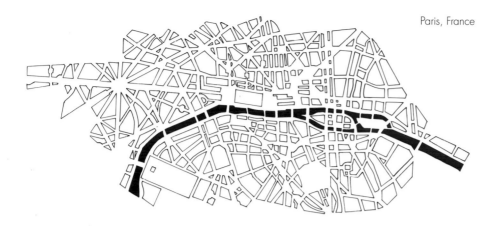

pentine course, a succession of more than twenty-five bridges stretching between the Pont National and the Pont Mirabeau creates arched frames for the water and provides viewing decks for the river and its decorated corridor.

Set against wide bodies of water or rivers as empty backdrops, bridges often have prominent urban positions in river cities. Impressive ones frequently become civic symbols: the Brooklyn Bridge in New York, the London Bridge (retired to Arizona), the Golden Gate Bridge in San Francisco, or the Rialto in Venice. Bridges are mediators, too. Rivers often segregate ideals, life-styles, or economic classes, and bridges help to foster connections between communities. The Pont Neuf links bureaucratic Paris with the intellectual Latin Quarter, the Cambridge Bridge connects pinstripe Boston with tweedy Cambridge, and the Ponte Sisto ties imperial Rome to the swarthy Trastevere.

To maximize precious urban space, bridges can also carry buildings on their decks. In Florence the Ponte Vecchio (Old Bridge) spans the Arno River with three low-slung arches. Gold dealers' boutiques (in times more medieval, they were less inviting pork butchers' counters) cling to the bridge like packages strapped onto the sides of an anchored barge. A secret passageway hidden beneath the attic links the Palazzo degli Uffizi on one bank with the more defensible Palazzo Pitti on the other bank, so that the ruling Medici family could safely retreat from the city in times of insurrection. Midway across the bridge, an arched gallery opens onto the Arno so that crossers can connect with a view of the water. It is a "somewhere-in-between" place, floating between the city and the river, the domain of humankind hovering over the domain of nature.

Bridge design depends, of course, on the nature of the gorge to be crossed as well as available materials and technologies. Early bridges were made of hefty stones and massive pilings to resist the lateral forces of strong currents. Bridges can span a river with many arches (the fifty-three arches of the Precious Belt Bridge in Suzhou were so expensive to construct that the Chinese governor had to donate his jade belt to the cause), or a few daring arches, like those of the Kintai Bridge in Hiroshima, Japan. Alberti recommended that "an odd number of arches will look pleasing, and also contribute to its strength. For in midstream the current, being farthest from contact with the bank, is least restricted, and the less restricted it is, the quicker and the more violently it rages."[45]

The result of developing technology and custom is a wide diversity of silhouettes, styles, and variations. Eventually steel and concrete replaced stone as the favored bridge-building material. Robert Maillart's amazing streamlined bridges span deep alpine gorges in Switzerland with just a thin line of elegantly arched concrete. Some bridges are complex erector-set assemblages of struts, beams, plates, cables, and rivets; others seem dis-

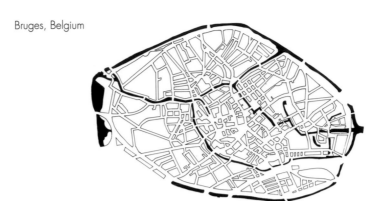
Bruges, Belgium

armingly ornamental and decorative. They can be very proper compositions, such as Richard Jones's Palladian bridge of 1755 in Bath (snugly inserted into the English naturalistic landscape of Prior Park), or very simple and whimsical bridges, meant only for feet, such as the painted tile bridges spanning the semicircular canal that sweeps through the Plaza de España in Seville.

The canal, or man-made river, is also an important connector and communicator. Canals can physically connect cities to bodies of water, lace together neighborhoods or districts, or link several cities in one line. Many canal cities began as towns ringed with circular moats, walls, and towers to defend against invasion. Medieval Bruges in Belgium was once within the confines of a canal-moat. Over time, canals were excavated from the main moat to allow access to the inner parts of the town, so that today the city is an interlocking puzzle of streets and narrow waterways.

Our penchant for canals was not even confined to our planet. For a long time, astronomers pondered the canal-like patterns on Mars as indicators of intelligent extraterrestrial life. Science-fiction fantasies of canal cities built by Martians captured Earthbound imaginations. In *Out of the Silent Planet*, C. S. Lewis described such a canal on Mars: "To the *handramit* itself there seemed no end; uninterrupted and very nearly straight, it ran before him, a narrowing line of colour, to where it clove the horizon with a V-shaped indenture."[46]

Back on Earth, nowhere is the canal and the world it creates more stirring than in Venice, the magical, mysterious city on water. Venice's confounding but surprisingly harmonious mishmash of contradictions and anomalies would have been grounds enough for a remarkable city; that the entire city is woven together with a web of water arteries instead of streets makes it all the more extraordinary. When Marco Polo visits Genghis

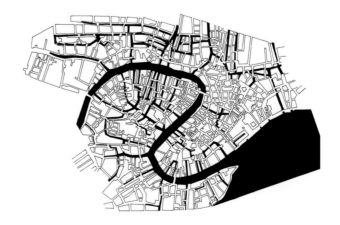
Venice, Italy

Khan in Italo Calvino's *Invisible Cities*, he captivates the emperor by eloquently describing forty imaginary cities, yet, near the end of his visit, Polo admits, "Every time I describe a city I am saying something about Venice [his hometown]." All of Polo's fictive cities are concealed somewhere within the Venetian labyrinth. They are "cities that can never be rebuilt or remembered," such as Zora, with "the melon vendor's kiosk, the statue of the hermit and the lion, the Turkish bath, the café at the corner, the alley that leads to the harbor," or Phyllis, with "the bridges over the canals, each different from the others: cambered, covered, on pillars, on barges, suspended, with tracery balustrades."[47] Visually intoxicating passageways wander among the aquatint palaces, whose walls lean unpredictably in and out. Dimly lit shrines filter incense up through the vaults against light streaming down from inaccessible portals. Bridges arch over the green waterways, crisscrossing into the distance, as the canals slowly bend out of sight. Often, the only sounds in the silent city come from the enameled black hulls of gondolas bumping against the brick walls. It is no wonder that Thomas Mann, in his masterpiece *Death in Venice*, called it the "most improbable of cities."[48]

The first canals in Venice were carefully designed to carry away filth and garbage by drawing water through the city to the sea. Over time, an organic network of interconnecting capillaries evolved. Buildings were packed in between the waterways, creating little islands, overlaid with a labyrinth of passages, squares, bridges, and sidewalks. The water pervades every setting in Venice; every district, every church, and every garden absorbs some hint or memory of the water-reflected light.

Venice is a decaying city—its beauty hides within its imperfections. The water in its canals is like arsenic (or worse, cholesterol) in arteries—a sinister substance that gradually undermines the foundations, dissolves the mortar, and rots the millions of piers that the city hovers on. Long ago, wooden pilings (perfectly preserved in salt water) were driven into the lagoon to support the city, but global warming and pollution from nearby factories and refineries have thrown the delicate balance out of kilter. Each time the water level shifts and exposes the tops of the piles, the foundations begin to rot and crumble, leaving marble pavements warped and dislocated by slow-motion earthquakes. At first glance, Venetian palazzi (medieval structures with Renaissance facades) are of unequaled splendor and richness, but rows of identical white columns supporting Byzantine arcades of slender pointed tracery may suddenly reveal one of their openings slightly out of line, a capital chipped away, or a column sinking because of a foundation in jeopardy. From the sea, canals invade the city, enforcing the tacit Venetian fate—to sink into the watery grave and complete the cycle.

Venice still reigns as the premier canal city, but she is not without company. In 1452 Marco Polo sent his countrymen the following description from China: "We shall tell you next of a large and very splendid city called Su-chau.... In this city there are fully 6,000 stone bridges, such that one or two galleys could readily pass beneath them."[49] Suzhou's canals began as a large rectangular trench enclosing the town. As the city grew and its spaces filled in with buildings, canals were extended from the main moat to infiltrate the tightly packed neighborhoods and districts.

Suzhou is a world of steamy primeval waterways lined with stairs leading to the water, where boats await. The old and vernacular village houses of plaster and wood collide with newer, intricately carved marble bridges ascending and descending with geometric precision, their half-moon arches coming full circle in the reflective water. It is a universe related to Venice through its water yet utterly foreign in terms of custom and

Suzhou, China

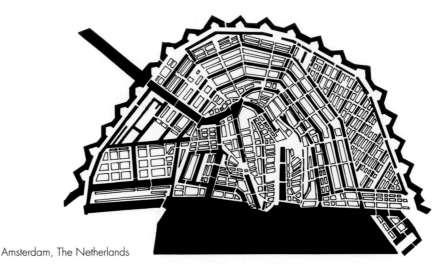

Amsterdam, The Netherlands

architecture. Unlike the Renaissance marble palaces that greet visitors who travel on Venice's canals, Suzhou's canals are lined with ramshackle houses with aged facades and blank walls. Inside though, the doors lead to magical interiors and precious gardens, all carefully composed and tended, which offer enclosed, private settings separated from the public world on the canals.

In contrast to the subtle organic pattern that prescribes the canal layouts in Venice, Bruges, or Suzhou, Amsterdam prefers a more regularized pattern, often described as a rigid semicircular spider's web of canals, dams, and locks. Amsterdam began as a simple town around a dam on the Amstel River. As the town grew, canals were built successively around the river in a series of concentric arcs. Each canal was longer than the last, and some had streets on each side and sites for warehouses, factories, and houses along the edges. Built on the resources of a bustling manufacture and trade, the canals allowed raw materials and goods to be moved quickly and cheaply around the city and out to port for international trade. The beneficiaries of the thriving economy built skinny Dutch houses—all lined with whitewashed window frames and mullions and frosted with eccentric attics and dormers elbowing for attention and space—along the canals. The water reflects the silvery Northern light into the scrubbed interiors, similar to the light Jan Vermeer masterfully recorded in nearby Delft. Like rows of playing cards, some buildings are simple and humble deuces, or sixes, sevens, and eights, but a few kings and the rare queen can be seen in palaces of quilted-brick patterns, with curled volute gables and entrances framed in elaborate pediments, columns, and moldings, all reflecting through the trees and into the connective water filling the liquid avenues.

In addition to linking geographical regions, architects can use tiny canals to conduct water around gardens or to imply symbolic connections. Like the axial canal at the Villa Lante, these canals are dramatically different in scale from the ones in Venice, Suzhou, or Bruges. In Seville, Spain, small canals laid out in a grid conduct water through the orchard in the Patio of the Oranges. At the mountaintop fortress of the Alhambra in Granada, miniature water canals (filled with renowned Sierra Nevada spring water) are an integral element of the gardens and courts. The walled complex was built by a succession of occupants, from thirteenth-century Moors to the sixteenth-century Holy Roman Emperor Charles V. The palace is a collection of towers, ramparts, and portals spread out along the spine of a hill. Within the massive bare walls are some of the most wonderfully ornate interiors, gardens, and fountains ever devised. Craftsmen painstakingly decorated walls and ceilings with cast plaster of geometric and plant patterns and elegant script whose fine detail catches every nuance of light and shadow. These shady interiors lead to sun-filled courts. In the famous Court of the Lions, four water canals converge at the center, where a pride of lions surround a fountain. These narrow canals, only inches deep, are sunken into the patio's smooth pavement. As they enter the court from the adjacent rooms, the canals flow through arcades of thin columns that support arbors of intricate plaster foliage to fill jets that squirt in the air. When the four canals reach the fountain, the water mingles in a ringed channel that catches spouts trickling from the twelve lions' maws. It is a garden paradise, but, unlike Eden, it receives life-giving water from the world beyond.

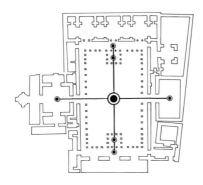

Court of the Lions, The Alhambra, Granada, Spain. Mid-14th century

Above the Alhambra, an exquisite garden complex named the Generalife (loosely translated as Garden of the Architect) also uses canals within its courts. In its south pavilion, the canal makes an axis for a garden arranged in narrow strips along the water's edge. Along the canal, berceaux squirt water into the air, where just enough pressure allows them to rise and then fall in narrow parabolas. The water jets crisscross in midair and fill the garden with the sound of raindrops. Arches frame the canal on each end. One is a Generalife entrance, the other frames a view of the distant Spanish hillsides. In another garden, and on an even smaller scale, water is carried down a staircase by means of hollow handrails. Water streams through the canals to follow the motion of people descending the staircase. Near the steps, valves can cause the handrails to overflow suddenly, so that the steps and the people walking up them are suddenly saturated.

Twentieth-century architects also have included figural canals in architectural compositions. Carlo Scarpa's Brion Cemetery of 1969, in San Vito d'Altivole, Italy, employs canals and water to suggest the connection between life and death. The cemetery is an intriguing complex of intricate geometries, centering on a chapel with a geode interior of sculpted concrete, bronze fixtures, oriental moon gates, and mechanical connections of ingenious detail. In the *campo santo*, a cluster of taut steel cables remind of life's delicate tension, always susceptible to the snap that instantly releases the spirit. Within a slender canal running along intersecting circles set in a wall, water slowly moves past the cables, across the green meadow, and toward the tomb. At the sarcophagus, the canal narrows into a thin strip and ends in a tiny circular pool.

Water that moves from the known to the unknown is central to Louis Kahn's Salk Institute in La Jolla, California, completed in 1965. Water enters the complex near a small garden orchard, where it pours from a block in a double weir. The water travels through a groove in the smooth travertine pavement, bisecting the court laid out between the twin laboratory buildings. As the blue canal cuts through the court in the morning, it creates a momentary impediment to crossing scientists; in the evening it becomes a trough of molten gold as its water catches light from the setting sun. At the edge of the court, the pavement drops off toward the ocean, and the canal seems to blend with infinity. According to Kahn, "I came up with the idea that what [Salk] wanted was a place of the *measurable*, which is a laboratory, and a place of the *unmeasurable*, which would be the meeting place."[50] The canal connects the known—scientists working in their laboratories with test tubes and instruments—to the unknown results and hopeful goals of their research summed up by the heroic Pacific horizon. A kind of modern-day Trevi, the courtyard and canal celebrate the biological cycle by incorporating the liquid cycle in the design, connecting a tiny portion of water to the rest of the world's liquid.

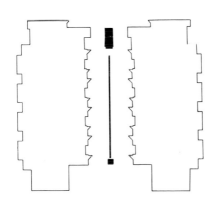

Louis I. Kahn. Salk Institute for Biological Studies, La Jolla, California. 1959–65

Above and opposite: Venice, Italy

Overleaf: River Walk, San Antonio, Texas

Lu Zhi, China

Opposite: Suzhou, China

Suzhou, China

Lower Slaughter, Wiltshire, England

Opposite: Bruges, Belgium

Opposite and above: Plaza de España, Seville, Spain

Overleaf: Ponte Vecchio, Florence, Italy

Pulteney Bridge, Bath, England

Palladian Bridge, Prior Park, Bath, England

Overleaf: Westminster Bridge and Big Ben, London, England

San Giorgio Maggiore and campanile, Venice, Italy

Opposite: Blackfriars Bridge and Saint Paul's, London, England

Pont Neuf and Île de la Cité, Paris, France

Opposite: Bangkok, Thailand

Overleaf: Near the Grand Canal, Suzhou, China

Hoover Dam, Arizona-Nevada border

Opposite: Kintai Bridge, Iwakuni, Japan

Solana, Southlake, Texas

Opposite: Salk Institute for Biological Studies, La Jolla, California

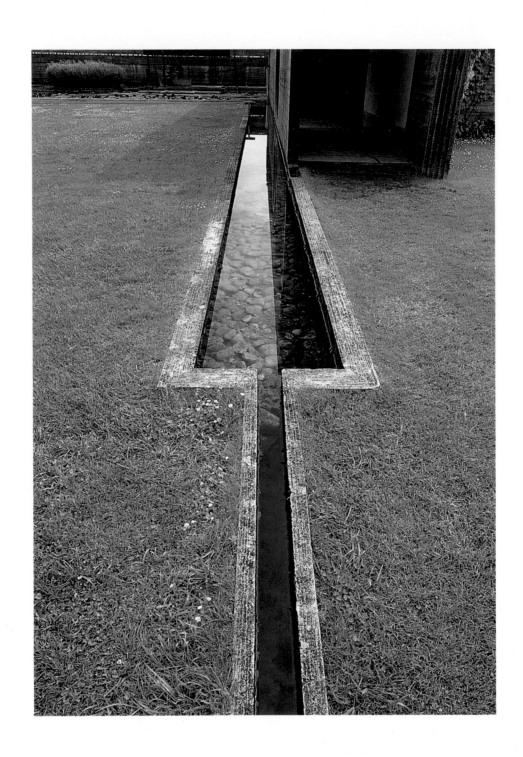

Brion Cemetery, San Vito d'Altivole, Italy

Court of the Lions, The Alhambra, Granada, Spain

STILL WATERS AND DREAMS:
REFLECTION AND COLLECTION

n northern France in 1845, a small stream flowed behind the Maison du Pressoir, one of the few prominent houses on the outskirts of what was then a modest country town. That year, however, the provincial government granted the following permit, which destined the town for fame: "[The] landowner . . . is authorized to divert the branch of the Epte River that crosses his land, which is situated in what is called Le Pressoir. Concerning . . . the pond, the water entering and leaving it may not be controlled by sluices but must be free flowing. . . . If this pond, which is for the cultivation of aquatic plants, should become a health hazard, the authorization granted . . . could be withdrawn."[51] Soon after, gardeners employed at the small estate diverted some of the stream's water to a small pond, forming a liquid mirror between the gardens and the stream.

Attention was lavished on the new pond. The owner drew up meticulous plans for the squad of gardeners and ordered exotic species of seeds and bulbs from around the world to be planted around the banks. The garden paths were carefully arranged to overwhelm the senses with chromatic fugues and aromatic juxtapositions. Tall evergreens shaded shorter fruit trees, and, below, mounds of white hydrangea engulfed top-heavy irises, spreading ferns, and red orchids. Carpenters built a Japanese footbridge over the pond's far end, where a weeping willow tree showered a veil of spikes and blades of light onto the water. Rushes and bamboo were started in the pond's shallows, and the grass on the banks was left to grow into an unkempt tangle. Since the pond was originally intended for "the cultivation of aquatic plants," the gardeners set out water lilies, which gathered into floating bunches and in the springtime bloomed into islands of pinks, reds, whites, and yellows. It should come as no surprise that the owner, Claude Monet, would spend his final years painting impressions of the transcendent water pond, his laboratory of color and light.

Monet began to paint his large-scale water-lily series in 1914 with the intention of bequeathing his last peaceful opus to the war-weary people of France. Just as Beethoven had struggled to compose his last symphonies with failing ears, Monet labored to paint his water lilies with eyes clouded with cataracts. The composer had had to draw sounds, notes, and rhythms from his memory; the painter had to reconstruct colors, hues, and intensities in his mind. After sixty years of painting the iridescent Seine, the Gare Saint-Lazare with steaming locomotives, misty Venetian cityscapes, and Rouen Cathedral dissolving in sunlight, Monet could rely on his instinctive habits of swirling brushstrokes and pigment ratios to allay his deteriorating vision. As a result, the pond at Giverny became,

Preceding pages: Jefferson
    Memorial, Washington, D.C.

Claude Monet
Nymphéas (Water Lilies). 1920–21
Oil on canvas, 6'5¹⁵⁄₁₆" × 19'6⅞"
    (198 × 596.6 cm)
The Carnegie Museum of Art, Pittsburgh
Acquired through the generosity of
    Mrs. Alan M. Scaife

in the words of another Frenchman, Gaston Bachelard, a "lake [that] takes all of light and makes a world out of it."[52]

In Monet's painted world, the still water reflects impressions of the bridge that hangs over it, the willow that descends to it, and the irises that surround it. Water lilies, sometimes green disks or sometimes red and purple whirls, float weightlessly on the surface. Climbing wisteria overtakes the bridge, entwining its railings and slats in blossoms from end to end, while vegetation covering the banks underneath obscures the transition from land to water. Mirrored lilies merge with the real ones so that where the water begins or ends is lost in myopic fusions of light, color, and form. A basin of liquid schizophrenia, the painted pool nervously shifts, holds, and releases the light, swaying constantly between misted illusions and polychrome clarity.

Monet's paintings have an unknowable depth and an indeterminate surface. Since the reflection covers the pond with a mirage of solid color, what hides beneath is elusive. Like Leonardo's water drawings, Monet's paintings are liquid seductions. They do not rely, however, on the sublime persuasions of fear and danger. Instead of containing violent waters, Monet created at Giverny a placid pool of reflection and collection—in it stir the still waters of dreams.

Unlike fountains and springs, rivers and canals, the pools and lakes of the world are not kinetic gushers or connectors; rather, they collect the water unleashed by rushing rivers or cyclical rains. The allegorical liquid that was pumped from the fountain's heart-source and distributed by the arterial rivers and canals rests in these basins. In his poem "On the Lake," Johann Wolfgang von Goethe describes the nuances of waters at rest:

> *And I suck fresh nourishment and new blood*
> *From the wide world;*
> *How gracious and kindly is Nature*
> *Who holds me to her breast!*
>
> *The waves rock our boat up and down*
> *To the rhythm of the oars,*
> *And soaring, cloud-capped mountains*
> *Meet us in our course.*
>
> *My eyes, why are you cast down?*
> *Golden dreams, will you return?*
> *Begone, dream, golden as you are;*
> *There is love here, and life too.*
>
> *On the waves float twinkling*
> *A thousand twinkling stars;*
> *Soft mists drink up*
> *The looming distances;*
>
> *The morning breeze wings around*
> *The shaded bay,*
> *And in the lake*
> *The ripening fruit is mirrored.*[53]

In this one poem, Goethe calls to mind three important qualities associated with still waters. First, they are receptacles or reservoirs contained under a horizontal surface. Second, the contemplative waters inspire "golden" dreams to fuel our imaginations. And last, they are the waters of reflection, returning to the eye a "thousand twinkling stars" and the "ripening fruit" of surrounding nature.

Ponds and pools are usually smaller basins that can be seen entirely from one vantage point and easily walked around. Lakes, traditionally, are larger bodies of water that can have shores stretching for miles and surface areas extending beyond the horizon. The ocean-like breadth of Lake Superior contrasts with the small Boston Common pool or tiny goldfish ponds in Tibetan monasteries. Some lakes, such as the Dead Sea or the Great Salt Lake, are remnants of ancient oceans and retain their salt long after their outlets have dried up. Lakes can be seasonal. In the Serengeti flats of Tanzania, some lakes collect only after weeks of the annual rains, sustaining entire ecosystems until the African sun dries the water back to fields of baked mud. Extinct lakes leave behind depressions that they once occupied, while volcanoes that no longer spew fiery lava sometimes fill with water, as in southern Oregon's Crater Lake, two thousand feet deep and six thousand feet above sea level. Lakes can also be created by damming rivers, as Lake Mead was in 1936 by its Art Deco container, Hoover Dam. Lakes can be destroyed by human intervention: Owens Valley at the base of Mount Whitney in California once supported a large lake, but it was drained and the water carried to Los Angeles by modern aqueducts.

For their pensive stillness and silent collection, still waters have traditionally represented the contemplative and pervasive "indwelling spirit" of nature residing in the forest. This was true for Western as well as Eastern minds, both ancient and modern. Virgil praised the lover of both science and nature, "who can live far from the crowded cities, among the hills and woods and rivers where men are less important than the indwelling spirits that outlive many human generations, but where men are closer to the real secrets of earth, their patient and expectant mother."[54] Virgil probably would have admired Henry David Thoreau, who adopted Walden Pond in eastern Massachusetts as a spiritual escape from society two thousand years later. Thoreau's descriptions of the lake are of particular interest: "The scenery of Walden is on a humble scale, and, though very beautiful, does not approach to grandeur, nor can it much concern one who has not long frequented it or lived by its shore; yet this pond is so remarkable for its depth and purity as to merit a particular description. It is a clear and deep green well, half a mile long and a mile and three quarters in circumference, and contains about sixty-one and a half acres; a perennial spring in the midst of pine and oak woods, without any visible inlet or outlet except by the clouds and evaporation."[55]

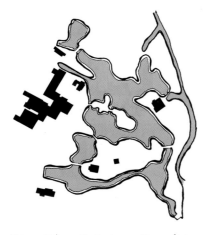

Katsura Palace, Kyoto, Japan. Begun first half 17th century

It is in the Orient that the concept of the indwelling spirit of nature has received the fullest attention. "People think that men alone have spirit," said Teng Ch'ien, a South Sung philosopher; "they do not realize that everything is inspirited."[56] Ponds and lakes in Oriental gardens were meant to be the souls of the world. Since the world was too large to be fitted completely around the perimeter of a small lake, gardeners selected miniature components of Japanese or Chinese landscapes (the Chinese word for landscape, *shanshui*, denotes "mountains and water") and arranged them around the watery stages. The lakes often have wildly undulating edges with paths and trails carefully planned for visitors to stroll in the wonders of nature. The Katsura Palace in Kyoto, begun in the first half of the seventeenth century as a country retreat for Prince Toshihito, is a masterpiece of this type of garden design. Fed by a river flowing through Kyoto, the garden's pond has an intricately winding bank, with many depressions, peninsulas, and islands. Gardeners were careful to develop several types of edges to the water—some overgrown with irises and bamboo, others built up with short stone walls, and still others paved with patterns of flat stones and moss—to create the feeling of marshes, cliffs, or beaches.

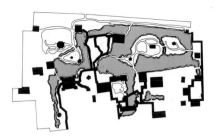

Zhouzheng Yuan, Suzhou, China. Early 16th century

Two Chinese gardens in the canal city of Suzhou use central ponds as ordering devices. In Zhuozheng Yuan (The Humble Administrator's Garden), a comparatively small pond (but in fact one of the largest in the city) seems larger than it actually is because its body is divided into several sections and its edges are built up with scaled-down detail. Begun during the early years of the Tang dynasty, the garden pond was gradually enlarged into its present shape by developments and additions made up to the sixteenth century.

The garden is an intricate world meant to be explored along paths that wind around the shores, through pavilions, and over the water on footbridges. Several large islands divide the rectangular lake into smaller zones, so that each pavilion has its own private reserve of pond, allowing the gardeners to create concealed views for visitors to discover as they walk along the sequenced paths. Long finger inlets penetrate the land and work in among the buildings. Zigzag bridges with tile roofs lead from the mainland to the islands, penetrating spatial layers of hanging willow branches, rocky shores (made to represent cliffs), views of distant towers, and diminutive temples. Thick white plaster walls, carved out with circular moon gates, frame the dense green gardens. Railings of Chinese Chippendale patterns, corrugated roof tiles, and delicate upturned eaves harmonize with nature's patterns of ribbed bamboo, screens of spiky leaves, and dappling water.

In the middle of the twelfth century, Shi Zhenghong built the garden of Wangshi Yuan (Master of the Nets), hidden behind high walls and an unassuming gate in the middle of crowded Suzhou. The pond in the center of the composition is one of the smallest in Suzhou, and its plan and details are much simpler than those of the Humble Administrator's Garden. A complex of interlocking halls surrounds the square pool, which has two small inlets extending from opposite corners. Its bank is made of large rocks stacked about three feet high, planted with bonsais, whose tortured, bent trunks frame the backdrop of white walls and centering roofs over little temples. Even though the garden is tiny, and enclosed behind high walls, the reflective depth of the pool helps to relieve the claustrophobia of the densely packed city. The passive collection of the still water brings the mind back to a contemplative state, away from the hustle and bustle of life in the exterior world of streets, markets, and canals.

The notion of lakes as sanctuaries and repositories for the indwelling spirit extended to the Eastern vision of heaven. When Amida Buddhism spread from India through the Orient, it brought new visions of a paradise for immortal souls a Pure Land beyond the sunset. According to the garden historian Loraine Kuck, this paradise has a "celestial palace on the edge of a lily-filled lake," where "the heavenly hosts await devout souls who are to be reborn to bliss on a blossom seat in this lake."[57] In Japan, the Phoenix Hall of the eleventh-century Byodo-in complex was built to signify such a palace and provide a place to meditate and worship. Yorimichi-no Michinaga's structure of 1053 stands on a stone island in the center of a lotus pond. The building consists of a monumental central pavilion with miniature aediculae on either side, which are linked by open loggias. Broad tile roofs sweep over the sumptuously decorated open-air structure, where a large stone Buddha housed under the central gable contemplates the pond and its scatter of lotuses. The water is used not only to reflect the building but also to isolate physically

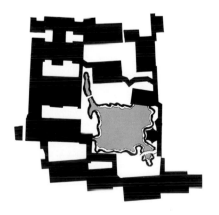

Wangshi Yuan, Suzhou, China. Begun 1140, restored 1770

Kinkaku-ji, Kyoto, Japan. Gardens begun early 15th century, pavilion rebuilt 1955

the heavenly mansion from the ordinary world, symbolically segregating the mortal from the immortal.

Stationary waters are natural reflectors; their mirrored surfaces absorb, repel, and refract their surroundings. Mirrored images of landscapes or buildings (whether the Tetons at Jenny Lake or Loire châteaux and their shallow moats) expand space by extending the foreground in a silver sheen or repeating the infinite depth of blue skies. Mirror Lake in the Sierra seems especially poignant for the stillness of its water, as captured by Ansel Adams in photographic images of striking detail and pristine monumentality. The edge of the pool at the Amandari Hotel in Bali, designed by Peter Muller, is lifted out of the ground so that its mirror-like plane is accentuated in a clean edge against the tropical sunsets and silhouetted palm trees. The brilliant sheen of water spills over the far edge (it is an optical illusion: though it seems to be spilling away into a great depth, the water actually falls only a few inches), pulling the surface as smooth as possible, while a thatched hut on slender poles seems to float in space over the broad saucer. In Costa Mesa, California, Peter Walker designed a pool that is divided by circular tracks of empty canals, making a perfect disk of gleaming silver. Convincing liquid-bound mirages at the Kinkaku-ji (Golden Temple) in Kyoto are betrayed only by the most minute ripples that flutter an eave or vibrate a column. Built in the fifteenth century (and then rebuilt in 1955 after falling victim to an arsonist), the gilded temple sits above Kyoko-chi (Mirror Lake), which extends to its base. The water reflects light off the gold-leaf walls and the undersides of the eaves, causing the whole building to glow.

Contemplative waters play an important role in mythology. Narcissus is perhaps the most famous example. When the dreamy youth sees his reflection for the first time in a forest pool, he falls hopelessly in love with himself. Trying to embrace his own image in the water, he falls into the pool and is literally drowned by his own desires. Ever since, the Greeks have regarded reflections in water as an omen of death. An Australian aboriginal tale explains the mysterious circular ponds on the continent's southern coast. According to legend, the pools formed when a male spirit angrily flung a handful of white-hot stars to Earth after he had been rejected by a female spirit hidden in the constellations. In the medieval English epic of King Arthur and the Knights of the Round Table, the charmed Excalibur rises out of the mysterious depths of a black lake. After Arthur's demise, the sword is returned to the Lady of the Lake (a female version of the indwelling spirit) and is lost forever in the coal-black depths. Centuries later, after Alice tumbles down the rabbit hole, she nearly drowns in a pool of her own tears in her dreamy tour of Lewis Carroll's Wonderland. Carl Jung, who spent his life probing the nature of dreams and the subconscious, linked some of his most profound experiences with water, returning in his old age to "memories afloat in a sea of vagueness." Jung's recollections of water were influenced by a lake: "My mother took me to the Thurgau to visit friends, who had a castle on Lake Constance. I could not be dragged away from the water. The waves from the steamer washed up to the shore, the sun glistened on the water, and the sand under the water had been curled into little ridges by the waves. The lake stretched away and away into the distance. The expanse of water was an inconceivable pleasure to me, an incomparable splendor. At that time the idea became fixed in my mind that I must live near a lake; without water, I thought, nobody could live at all."[58]

Throughout history lakes have been settings for cities and towns where people could live near the water. The Aztec capital, Tenochtitlán (now buried beneath Mexico City), was built in the center of a lake with an elaborate system of walls, dams, and dikes to pro-

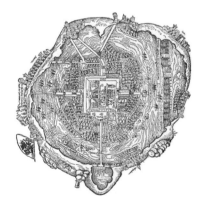

Tenochtitlán. Map of Mexico City from Cortés's second letter to Charles V. c. 1520

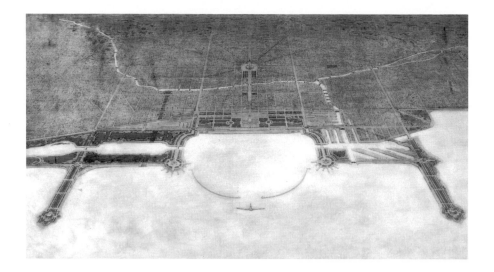

tect the floating city from flooding. When the conquistador Bernal Díaz del Castillo arrived in Tenochtitlán, he marveled at the great pyramid of Huitzilopochtli and the palace of Moctezuma II, and he reported that one could move around the city only by the use of canoes or wooden drawbridges that connected the buildings. Garrison Keillor's fictive Lake Wobegon may not be filled with enchanting visions of architecture, but the small lake still provides a place to call home within the daunting tundra of Minnesota.

Wobegon's humble Main Street cannot really compare with Chicago's grand Michigan Avenue, where a wall of corporate skyscrapers send office views out over the water of Lake Michigan. Once an East West stopover, Chicago is now a major lake city rising from the flat plains of glacier-smoothed Illinois. Buckingham Fountain, which blasts lake water into the air at the centerpoint of the city's connection with Lake Michigan, was once the focus of plans to tie the city majestically to the lake. The 1893 World's Columbian Exposition (mostly demolished) and Daniel Burnham's 1910 city plans (largely unrealized) envisioned a lake ceremonially bonded with the city. Diagonal avenues were to extend into the great prairies from monumental civic buildings lining the water, while a Beaux Arts harbor, handsomely framed by lighthouses, tree-lined piers, and fountains, would have implanted a formal arrangement on the natural lake edge.

Many times, in the absence of lakes or ponds, designers and builders have made pools to imitate the natural ones. Artificial pools can mimic nature closely or even embellish it by exaggerating edges, shapes, or surroundings. The chief elements for naturalistic pools are amorphous shapes with soft and untrained banks that connect harmoniously to the neighboring terrain.

As difficult as it is to reproduce the random quality of nature's hand, the artificial pond that the emperor Gomizuno'o-tenno built at the garden of Shugaku-in outside Kyoto in 1652 is astonishingly convincing. Because the pond was sited on a hillside (instead of in a valley, where water could fill a natural depression), the lower edges had to be built up with earthen walls to create a bowl so that the collecting water could find its horizontal equilibrium. Paths follow the shore through the forest garden, slowly winding under branches and shrubs and emerging around grassy hills and fields. Since sections of the shoreline disappear into the forest, the water seems especially inviolable and secluded. Undulations in the shoreline elaborate and advance the foreground, while overhanging limbs, the uninterrupted plane of water, and a distant aedicula enrich the perspective. Portions of the bank are planted with high hedges and trees to enclose the pond and visu-

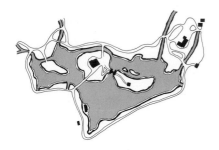

Shugaku-in, Kyoto, Japan. Mid-17th century

ally strengthen its edge; other sections are left open to the wide views of the distant mountains and nearby rice paddies. The space afforded by the reflection as well as the panoramas of the distant peaks provide a visual outlet for the enclosed setting.

The importance of natural-water features in English gardens was eloquently emphasized by Thomas Whately in his *Observations on Modern Gardening* (1772): "[Water] accommodates itself to every situation; is the most interesting object in a landscape, and the happiest circumstance in a retired recess; captivates the eye at a distance, invites approach, and is delightful when near; it refreshes an open exposure; it animates a shade; chears [*sic*] the dreariness of a waste, and enriches the most crouded [*sic*] view: in form, in style, and in extent, [it] may be made equal to the greatest compositions, or adapted to the least: it may spread in a calm expanse, to sooth the tranquillity of a peaceful scene; or hurrying along a devious course, add splendor to a gay, and extravagance to a romantic, situation."[59] Water achieves no less at the estate of Stourhead in Wiltshire, where an artificial lake became the setting for a compelling storybook landscape. In the mid-eighteenth century, Henry Hoare, the garden's first owner, blocked off the river Stour with a land dam. Collecting water inundated the valley and formed a pond in the shape of a three-pointed star, as if it had been pinched by giant fingers from three sides. Intent on creating a well-mannered landscape, the English gardeners set out to give nature a manicure, using the lake as the center of the composition of green slopes, sinuous banks, and backdrops of deciduous forests and meadows rising to meet the sky. Trees that would take a hundred years to mature and achieve their full effect were planted around the lake and on the hills, and an eclectic collection of temples was built in the youthful gardens.

In a plan reminiscent of Shugaku-in, gravel trails follow the banks of the three-pronged lake and weave through the exaggerated landscape of planned perspectives, drawing out the perimeter and making it seem larger in the mind. Unlike the Eastern gardens, however, Stourhead's paths are also interwoven with a literary narrative based on Virgil's *Aeneid*. Things of the mind are layered over the primarily visual, imparting an additional level of meaning for people versed in classical literature. Visitors follow in the footsteps of the ancient hero along a network of trails that wander across sunny lawns to dark hollows. Shady porticoes of granite Ionic columns open onto soft hillsides, and paths lead to a summit of the hill, where the composition can be seen from a bird's-eye vantage point. Near the lake, the gravel path descends into a gaping black hole encrusted with rocks and hardened lava. Below the lake is a grotto, where Alexander Pope's warning is spelled out for the invading spelunkers:

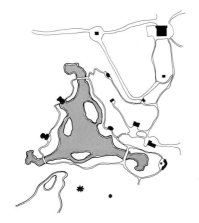

Henry Hoare. Stourhead Gardens, Wiltshire, England. Begun 1741

> *Nymph of the Grot these sacred springs I keep*
> *And to the murmur of these waters sleep;*
> *Ah! Spare thy slumbers, gently tread the cave,*
> *And drink in silence or in silence lave.*

Like Monet's pond, a liquid mirror above conceals this haunted world of stalagmites below the stirring waters.

The designer's goal was to make Stourhead the garden equivalent of Nicolas Poussin's and Claude Lorrain's painted picturesques by using visual perspectives and spatial layering to create garden scenes with a painterly depth. Mature oaks in the foreground pull the picture plane forward and provide leafy frames for the shimmery water floor. The flat plane of water occupies the middle ground and deepens the perspective by

Nicolas Poussin
Landscape with Two Nymphs. 1651
Oil on canvas, 46½ × 70½"
(118.1 × 179.1 cm)
Musée Condé, Chantilly

pushing the background away from the observer—hills and trees gradually fade into the hazy atmosphere across the lake, and temples are set along axial vistas. Through the tree branches, scenes of the arched bridge frame the shrunken Pantheon across the lake, carefully placed at an angle to enhance the perspective; another vista connects the Temple of Flora, set within a pocket of foliage, with a miniature Temple of Baalbek. All that is missing from the pastoral landscape, its tranquil water, and idyllic temples are Bacchanalians reveling in the sunshine to complete the allusion to *et in arcadia ego*.

Like rivers and canals, artificial pools and lakes are not limited to natural shapes with picturesque intentions. To distinguish their pools from natural forms, some designers opt for abrupt transitions from ground to water. The shapes are usually geometrically regular. Squares, rectangles, circles, and, in twentieth-century California, kidney beans are popular. Though some pools are not meant for contact, artificial pools are used most often for swimming. One of the most striking is Arquitectonica's Pink House pool, which is a tropical composition of Miami palms, azure blues, glass blocks, and neon-pink walls.

In its capacity to reflect, the artificial pool can be a compelling compositional device, such as the famous pool at the Taj Mahal, which establishes its important linear axis. Some of the most awe-inspiring pools were designed by French landscapers to create an illusion of infinite distance stretching through the formal gardens into the landscape. At Vaux-le-Vicomte, André le Nôtre set the primary canal on a *cross axis* to expand east and west, pierce the walls of the garden, and disappear into the forest. Wide allées, expansive lawns, and shallow pools (repeating the infinite skies) radiate from the palace in perspectives that vanish into distant points, reflecting and configuring sublime visions of the landscape.

Pools can also create magical effects of a different kind. The 1984 World's Fair in New Orleans featured an artificial pond inhabited by an enormous papier-mâché alligator, who watched as reptilian cohorts chased a flock of pelicans up the Wonder Wall to the hub of the world's largest Ferris wheel. At nightfall, the scene was made still more exciting by thousands of blinking colored lights, instantly multiplied by the reflective water.

Both naturally and geometrically shaped pools and lakes are integral elements in the design of Washington, D.C. Two early plans for the city (made when the area was still a

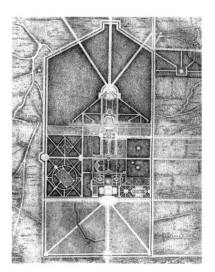

Israel Sylvestre
Plan of Vaux-le-Vicomte Showing Water Canal. c. 1661

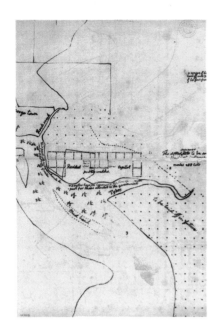

Thomas Jefferson
Washington, D.C. March 1791
Sketch, 15¼ × 9⅝" (38.7 × 24.5 cm)
The Library of Congress, Washington, D.C.

forest) used Tyber Creek and the Potomac River, in very different ways, as the organizing spine of open space. Thomas Jefferson's sketchy plan suggested a public area open to the water, with bays of land facing the water for the presidential mansion and the Capitol. Pierre L'Enfant's famous 1791 plan for the city—combining Versailles's regal pomp with the fancy diagonal avenues of Sistine Rome—was much grander. He planned to extend a canal from Tyber Creek past the presidential lawn, along the north side of the Mall. At the base of the Capitol, L'Enfant intended to build a monumental waterfall, "letting the Tiber return in its proper channel by a fall which issuing from under the base of the Congress building may there form a cascade of forty feet heigh [*sic*] or more than one hundred waide [*sic*] which would produce the most happy effect."[60]

L'Enfant's scheme was selected for the design of the nation's capital, but the canal and cascade were never built. Nevertheless, as the city developed over the next two hundred years, water was reincorporated into the design, based on the idea of water as a spatial organizer. Of particular importance is the core of the city, the central Mall (laid out between James Renwick's Smithsonian Castle and its assortment of related museums), where the Capitol gazes from its hilltop perch over a quadrilateral reflecting pond. Over time, monumental landmarks and pools were built to decorate the public green. The formal water arrangement begins with a pool with semicircular ends situated at the base of the white obelisk of the Washington Monument. Next, a rectangular Reflecting Pool stretches two thousand feet toward Henry Bacon's Lincoln Memorial (dedicated in 1922) and is flanked by double rows of elms. The flat plane of water leads to a monumental flight of marble stairs that ascends to the figure of Abraham Lincoln, who observes the gatherings in the nation's collective backyard, his back turned to the Potomac River.

The Mall crouches in the arm of the Potomac, where a small canal feeds the Tidal Basin due south of the White House. The water extends to the Jefferson Memorial (dedicated in 1943), whose marble facade, shallow pediment, and silken dome repeat in the water. The soft curves of the naturalistic shoreline complement John Russell Pope's

Pierre-Charles L'Enfant
Plan of the City of Washington, D.C.
Engraving by Thackara & Vallance,
        Philadelphia, 1792

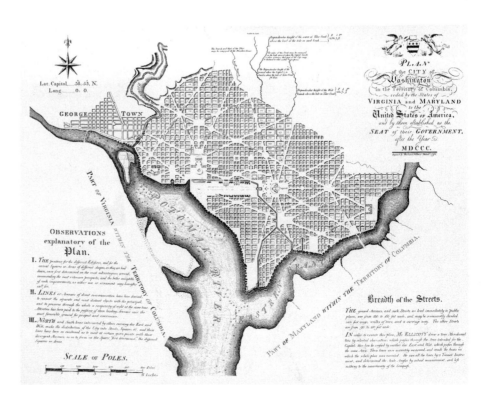

round structure, as the rectangular pools converge in straight lines to the blockier Lincoln Memorial. Apart from the occasional paddleboat, the Tidal Basin presents a wide open space with an unimpeded view of the distant memorial. In the springtime, the effect is made still more extraordinary when the famed cherry trees lining the shores and gentle knolls fill the reflection with forests of pink blossoms.

These waters provide a setting for important occasions associated with the capital— marches, speeches, Fourth of July fireworks (when Henry Bacon received the National Gold Medal in architecture, admiring students towed him on a barge down the length of the Reflecting Pool)—and reflect not only the physical monuments but also the dreams of the heroes for whom they were built, as well as our national aspirations.

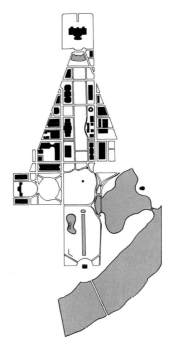

Washington, D.C.

In a sense, *to contemplate* means to look both back to the past and toward the future. Mythic proportions and classically heroic aspirations inflate the two swimming pools at San Simeon—William Randolph Hearst's palatial mountaintop retreat. This California acropolis was designed and built during the second quarter of this century by Julia Morgan (the world's first prominent female architect) as an elaborate playground for Hearst and his glamorous circle of socialites, movie stars, and moguls. Underneath the tennis courts, Hearst and Morgan built an indoor pool in the style of the ancient Roman baths. Nearly every surface of the cavernous shell, including the basin of the pool, glints with millions of blue mosaic chips and gilded overlay. Light pours in through French windows and skylights and, in the evening, alabaster lamps emit a warm glow.

The outdoor pool was designed as a tribute to Neptune, god of the oceans. Its deep basin, shaped like a broad keyhole, is filled with nearly invisible water—crystal clear and sparkling. Situated on a terrace below the main house, the pool cants out on a ledge overlooking the Pacific Ocean. An antique Corinthian temple facade, which Hearst purchased in Europe, dismantled, and carted to California, stands between the pool and the hills. Ionic colonnades surround the elliptical basin, and fancy marble stairs switch-back up the terraces. Greek geometric patterns of blue and black inlaid tile decorate the container of the pool, with stone ladders that descend into the thousands of gallons of water. In this grand liquid ballroom, Hollywood Olympians lucky enough to be granted coveted weekend invitations (Clark Gable, Greta Garbo, Douglas Fairbanks, Marion Davies, for instance) swam high above the mortal realm fanning out below. With its antique trappings, the pool recalls the past while the views out toward the infinite skies inspire imaginative visions into the unknown. Its still water, like Giverny's, at one time contained something more than itself. Looking out over the terrace, however, one realizes that this pool, propped up with its Olympian costumes, defers to the ocean waters stretching toward the horizon.

Wateridge Marketing Pavilion, San Diego, California

Opposite: Washington Monument, Washington, D.C.

Plaza Tower, Costa Mesa, California

Opposite: Wateridge Marketing Pavilion, San Diego, California

Carrasco House, Bornos, Spain

The Pink House, Miami, Florida

Overleaf: World's Fair Wonder Wall, New Orleans, Louisiana

Roman Pool, Hearst Castle, San Simeon, California

Opposite: Court of the Myrtles, The Alhambra, Granada, Spain

Neptune Pool, Hearst Castle, San Simeon, California

Opposite: Roman Pool, Hearst Castle, San Simeon, California

King's Bath, Bath, England

Opposite: Roman Bath and Abbey, Bath, England

Claude Monet's water garden, Giverny, France

Stourhead Gardens, Wiltshire, England

Claude Monet's water garden, Giverny, France

Opposite: Shugaku-in, near Kyoto, Japan

Overleaf: Byodo-in, Kyoto, Japan

Zhouzheng Yuan, Suzhou, China

Opposite: Temple West Garden, Suzhou, China

Reflection of Kinkaku-ji, Kyoto, Japan

Amandari, Ubud, Bali

SEAS OF INFINITY,
ISLANDS OF ISOLATION

scension Thursday was an important day in eighteenth-century Venice. In fact, it might be called the most important holiday for the Republic, since every year, its leader—the supreme doge—would offer his hand in marriage in an explosion of pageantry.

Thousands would congregate in the Piazza San Marco, the famous urban heart of Venice, jammed for the celebration with festival booths and tents. At the edge of the piazzetta, the doge would lightly step onto the gilded *bucintoro* (a ceremonial barge) waiting for his departure to the wedding ceremony. Every seaworthy craft participated in a magnificent regatta in pursuit of the *bucintoro:* ships from the East with masts draped in yards of white sail, war boats displaying their colors in resplendent pride, barges carrying costumed Venetians, and slender gondolas negotiating narrow paths between the larger vessels. The wedding barge would make its way across the lagoon, slipping through the Palladian Giudecca and sailing past the Lido toward the island outskirts, with Venice fading into a misty skyline in the distance.

Out in the open waters of the Adriatic, the doge would solemnly rise from his floating throne and invoke the Latin words that his predecessors had spoken in exactly the same way on Ascension Thursdays for the past six hundred years: "Desponsamus te, mare, in signum veri perpetuique dominii."[61] He would then flip a golden wedding ring into the sea, where it would quickly sink into the depths. The sea it turns out, was the Ascension

Preceding pages:
Tokyo Sea Life Park, Japan

Canaletto
The Bucintoro Returning to the Molo on Ascension Day. Before 1731
Oil on canvas, 30¼ × 49⅜"
(76.8 × 125.4 cm)
Royal Collection, Saint James's Palace
© Her Majesty Queen Elizabeth II

Thursday bride, and the words, "We wed you, O sea, as a sign of true and perpetual dominion," were the vows that betrothed the doge, and the republic of islands, to the sea. No city would ever be so intimately connected with the sea. Proud Venetians assumed that their empire would last forever, and so this wedding ceremony signified a marriage of everlasting significance, unlimited power, and inexhaustible resource. What better way to express perpetual fidelity to the Venetian tradition than by a pairing of opposites: infinite sea and finite island?

Contradictions illustrate oceans' and seas' incredible power to overwhelm and astonish. Astronomers inform us that the Earth's nurturing oceans may be unique in the hostile universe. Our planetary anomaly underscores the scientific fact that life simply would not exist without water. In fact, our evolutionary history began in the oceanic soup; for millennia, the seas have incubated life in their warm waters. But even as the ocean sustains life, it also drowns life with its awesome power. As it relentlessly cleaves continents, swallows ocean liners, and batters defenseless coasts, the sea exposes the frailty of anything placed in its way. A foremost poetic image is of the watery eternal, exemplified in Percy Bysshe Shelley's

> *Unfathomable Sea! whose waves are years!*
> *Ocean of Time, whose waters of deep woe*
> *Are brackish with the salt of human tears!*
> *Thou shoreless flood which in thy ebb and flow*
> *Claspest the limits of mortality,*
> *And, sick of prey, yet howling on for more,*
> *Vomitest thy wrecks on its inhospitable shore!*
> *Treacherous in calm, and terrible in storm,*
> *Who shall put forth on thee,*
> *Unfathomable Sea?*[62]

The seemingly infinite waters confront human mortality and smallness, but their extensive presence on Earth surrounds us with a feeling of immediacy, intimacy, and belonging. As it rhythmically waves onto beaches around the world, crashes in white water against desolate cliffs, or gently ventures into safe harbors, the eternal ocean comes into physical contact with land and humanity. People swim in it, cross it on voyages, walk on its beaches, explore its depths, and seek to conquer it. Jules Verne, who told the story of a terrifying encounter with a menacing octopus in *Twenty Thousand Leagues Under the Sea*, cried out: "Yes; I love it! The sea is everything. It covers seven-tenths of the terrestrial globe. Its breath is pure and healthy. It is an immense desert, where man is never lonely, for he feels life stirring on all sides. The sea is only the embodiment of a supernatural and wonderful existence. It is nothing but love and emotion; it is the 'Living Infinite,' as one of your poets has said."[63]

Oceans and seas are incredibly huge volumes of water that move within themselves. Waves provide the most striking visual impression of the uncontrolled power of the sea. Seasons, tides, coastal geography, and atmospheric conditions all affect the action of waves—the mesmerizing disorder of water surging forward and flowing back on itself in an elliptical path of constantly changing patterns and rhythms. An important aspect of waves is their sound, which can range from the crashing of surf into rocks to the drone of water lapping on sandy beaches. Though waves are seldom more than twenty-five feet high, storms or earthquakes can send a tsunami (tidal wave) across the surface with a height of sixty feet or more: "Waves striking the shore of Tierra del Fuego can be heard for twenty miles. Spray from a storm wave has been hurled to the top of a lighthouse nearly 200 feet above sea level. The force of waves striking the shore can be measured, and has been found to reach three tons per square foot."[64]

Just as the boundless oceans frame our days, they are also the magnificent beginning and end of the water cycle, international thresholds between water and land. Their endless volumes continually absorb fresh water from rains, rivers, and streams. At the same time, their broad surfaces supply outgoing water through evaporation, sending the water back to land where springs resume the process down the line. In the bay surrounding the Japanese island of Miyajima, the Torii Gate represents one such threshold. In traditional Shinto architecture, the *torii* (Japanese for "gateway") delineates sacred temple boundaries. Stepping through the simple gate represents the ritual transition from the profane exterior to the sacred interior. Instead of being built over a temple entrance, however, this torii is placed in the sea; the cross beams frame the inland mountains from one direction and water from the other. Anchored piers (that act as yardsticks for the bay tides) rise out of the salty water and impose something of a recognizable human scale on the scaleless.

Deep, mysterious worlds, of which we can only ever glimpse a fraction, stir curiosity for the oceans and the misunderstood creatures that inhabit them. The aquarium, an important genre in oceanic architecture, reflects these attractions. At the Seattle Aquarium, Bassetti, Norton, Metler & Rekevics designed an extraordinary tank for exotic, polychrome fish, graceful but menacing stingrays, and beady-eyed sharks. The tank hovers above a Pantheon-like dome whose coffers have been popped out and replaced with glass, the oculus framed with a giant glass cornea, and the entire space above filled with water. Fish swim overhead and all around, while the light passing through the tank bathes the room in an aquamarine glow. In the Marine World Aquarium in Vallejo, California, a glass tunnel with a moving sidewalk lets visitors pass through a tank inhabited by an assortment of sharks. Down the coast, in Monterey Bay, the design team of Esherick, Homsey, Dodge, and Davis converted an old canning factory (on John Steinbeck's Cannery Row) into an aquarium that blends into the town's rustic factory architecture. Concrete sheds arranged on a wharf extending into the harbor incorporate the bay's water for outdoor exhibits of sea lions and otters. Instead of being gutted, chopped, and canned inside, the fish specimens swim in an aquatic asylum behind plate-glass displays. Exposed pipes, ducts, and valves on the interior add to the feeling of being inside a factory or a ship, and walls of glass frame brilliant displays of gleaming sardines and translucent jellyfish.

On the Atlantic coast in Baltimore, the National Aquarium (designed by Cambridge Seven in 1981) is a festive celebration of the marine world disguised in naval camouflage. Its sheet-metal facades and concrete walls are decorated with super-large graphics, steamship portals, a gangway entrance, smokeless smokestacks, and neon swells. Inside, gigantic concrete holding tanks contain the marine environments, balconies provide viewing platforms for the displays, and escalators zigzag through the space under reflective ceilings that glow from turquoise pools on the floor. On the upper deck, a pyramidal greenhouse provides a light-filled contrast to the darker galleries below deck.

A freshwater pool (whose surface is higher than sea level) surrounds the entrance to Yoshio Taniguchi's Tokyo Sea Life Park and seems to extend to the sea. Unlike in most aquaria, here visitors ride escalators down into the fish galleries, suggesting descent into the mysterious depths. A delicate glass jellyfish hovers above the entrance and in the evening glows like a phosphorescent deep-sea organism. In the distance, stationary tents imitate sails on the water while mist machines exhale fog into the skies, creating surreal marine compositions.

Another form of architecture exclusive to the ocean realm is the lighthouse, whose unique shapes are recognizable anywhere in the world. The paradigm of lighthouses is the famous beacon at Cape Hatteras in North Carolina, capped off in 1870 at an impressive height of one hundred and eighty feet. Its light is held aloft by a tall, tapering tube painted in black-and-white barbershop spirals. (Lighthouses were painted with distinctive stripes and patterns so that sailors could identify their positions along the coast during daytime.) The lighthouse in Newport, Oregon, assumes Puritanical humility: its tower is starched in anonymous white plaster; its no-nonsense opening is simple and its handsome detailing understated so as not to spoil or compete with the pristine landscape of the coast. Massive walls laid out in a circular plan resist the wind and sea; at top, the rotating beam sends pulses of light into the dark void, while the humble tender's quarters at the bottom suggest a lonely, hermit-like existence always subject to the challenges of living so close to the sea. By contrast, in Baltimore Harbor a Hawthornian-scarlet lighthouse sits next to an old factory, calling to mind seedy ports made dangerous by pirates and drunken sailors. The lighthouse illuminates the harbor in order to guide ships safely into dock. Taking advantage of the sheltered harbor, (like many Chesapeake lighthouses) it is not a virtuous ivory tower but a squat wooden drum perching on rickety stilts.

From Annapolis to Lisbon, Portsmouth to Sydney, San Francisco to London, ports and harbors are places that exist by definition at the edge of continents or islands, thereby in intimate contact with the sea. The nature of this connection—of the gradual or sudden transition from land to water—affects the ways people build around the edges to accommodate the activities associated with harbors. Wharves and piers provide places for people to board moored vessels, warehouses store cargo arriving or leaving, and quays and boardwalks allow pedestrians to walk near the edge.

Portofino, Italy, and its harbor are inseparable. Before the advent of modern tourism, the town was a sleepy fishing port, built literally on the edge of the water around a small harbor in the Ligurian coast. Taking maximum advantage of the sheltered cove, the town turns its face to the water with a minimum of separation and distance. Sturdy houses line the water's edge, forming a habitable retaining wall between the mountain and the sea. The solid wall of dwellings is collaged with an assortment of tinted stuccos, made neighborly by rows of shops along the bottom and uniformly painted green shutters above. Windows and balconies simply appear where needed, defying any ordered arrangement. There are no spaces between the wall of houses, and the only separation between the town and the water is a narrow sidewalk, laid out in a gentle arc that leads into the town square. The town's central piazza is adjacent to the water (as in Venice), with three sides defined by buildings and the fourth edge gradually sloping into the sea. Its minimal edge against the water is delineated by a flat strip of stones and is lined with iron mooring bollards that have been worn to rounded shapes by constant exposure to the elements. Slender streets wind through the town up the hill, where glimpses of the blue water appear through narrow alleys, pungent salt air sweeps over rooftop gardens, and sounds of the tides and gulls echo through the wooden roof of the striped church there. Up on the hill, the connection to the infinite and uncontrolled is maintained through views beyond the harbor to the Mediterranean Sea, while the calm inlet below promotes peace of mind.

Hong Kong has an equally intimate connection with the water, but its scale can be compared to Portofino's as that of a whale to a minnow. Portofino's quaint sea facade is replaced along Hong Kong's edge with hundreds of financial high rises. Hong Kong's natural rhythms are overshadowed by industrial and economic cacophonies that crowd its port with freighters, steamers, and tankers (making it the busiest port in the world) and its streets with honking cars and throngs of people. Hong Kong is a port of fascinating juxtapositions, old and modern. For all of its sleek banks, towering hotels, and miles of neon, a more human dimension manages to surface as well. Vendors with bushels of string beans fill the streets, neighborhood balconies support clotheslines, and small fishing boats work their way among the tankers and cruise ships. From the bay at night, the city's crystalline electric displays are reflected in the water and intensified by the black backdrop of Victoria Peak and the inland mountains. Towers with millions of fluorescent office lights, joined by tinier lighted windows dashed like salt across the mountainside and strings of lights draped across anchored ships, sparkle in the black water.

Regardless of their size or location, all ports share a common phenomenon. People who live in and visit harbor cities invariably need to approach as close as physically possible to the water's edge, from a dock, a rocky outcropping, a platform deck, or a moored ship. It is one of the most important aspects of the human relationship to the sea—to be able to confront its eternity within the context of the limited. "But look!" Herman Melville exults in *Moby Dick*, "here come more crowds, pacing straight for the water, and seemingly bound for a dive. Strange! Nothing will content them but the extremest limit of the land; loitering under the shady lee of yonder warehouses will not suffice. No. They must get just as nigh the water as they possibly can without falling in. And there they stand—miles of them—leagues."[65]

Piers, boardwalks, and decks accommodate this need in several different ways and must be designed with extreme care. The nature of the pier is to extend the edge of land to a point of immediate contact with water—to provide the exciting nearness of something that is limitless, for Gordon Cullen an act of "mental leaning out over."[66] Depending on its method of separation, materials, and distance from the water, each treatment affords the pedestrian different levels of contact with the water.

Pier 7 in San Francisco is a pedestrian boardwalk that, instead of running parallel to the beach (as most East Coast examples do), juts out into the bay. Concrete footings elevate the wooden plank floor several feet above the water, and high metal railings prevent tourists from falling into the bay. Streetlamps line each side, and benches provide places for people to contemplate the neighboring hills of the Bay area. The Itsukushima Shrine at Miyajima (across from the Torii Gate) has a red loggia of elaborate joinery and carving that forms a remarkably civilized edge of the bay. Floor planks and tatami mats are raised just inches from the surface of the water and are separated from it by only a narrow space and a wooden railing, so there is a feeling that the entire building is floating on the water.

Rarely expected to withstand devastatingly violent weather, piers in the open sea are built simply so they can be rebuilt quickly after storms, or are built of such permanence as to defy attempts by the sea to sweep them away. In the West Indies, or the San Juan Islands, docks (miniature piers) accommodate yachts and departing scuba divers. The best ones have spaces between the floorboards so that one can see the water lapping underneath yet remain suspended safely over it. Cabanas at their ends provide umbrellas to escape the sun, and the absence of barriers affords a place to dangle the feet in the water.

Few people would think of dangling their feet in the water from the jetty curving into the sea at Lyme Regis in West Dorset, England. Its deck is lifted high above the icy surf by a massive stone base that resists the Atlantic's constant hammering. Railings along the top are made of thin pipes so that the water can crash through and, at the same time, provide people with grips for braving the waves.

Strong winds from the ocean and dramatic views to the horizon characterize the northern California coast where the Sea Ranch Condominiums were built in the mid-1960s. The coastline is dramatically beautiful, and often dangerously abrupt, as it falls off into the water from cliffs hundreds of feet high. Beaches among the deep coves are accessible by stair towers tucked in natural pockets in the cliffs, and, offshore, bits of the continent make small islands, occupied on most days by sunbathing sea lions. Beyond the coastal road, the hills have been worn to a smooth roundness. Their meadows are usually kept golden by the frugal rainfall and are separated and protected from the violent coastal winds by hedgerows of Monterey cypress. Barns dating from the ranch's agricultural past dot the landscape. Their post-and-beam structures of heavy timbers frame simple volumes and silhouettes, with shed roofs slanting down toward the sea. Fog is a frequent factor as it banks in from the sea in huge fronts, sweeps over the cliffs, and moves inland to sift through the meadows. On bright, clear days, however, the coast is bathed in a light that can cause amazing color changes in the sea, ranging from deep blues, greens, and purples to shimmering golds and reds ignited by the setting sun.

The Sea Ranch was intended to be a model coastal community. Lawrence Halprin's environmental analysis and master plan of the ten-mile stretch of coast was founded on one principle—that neither buildings nor people should dominate the landscape; rather, they should live in harmony with it. Trees, views, paths, and meadows were not regarded as things to be cut down, destroyed, or bulldozed indiscriminately to make way for buildings. As the community evolved, strict design codes mandating the shapes, siting, and materials of the new houses were established in order to develop a consistent aesthetic based on the vernacular architecture.

The first cluster of condominiums (designed by Moore, Lyndon, Turnbull, and Whitaker) takes its cue from the earlier barns. The outlines are generally simple—mostly geometrical assemblages capped with shed roofs. Entrance to the condominium site is by a pathway through a cypress allée, the trees grown together overhead after a quarter of a century. At the end of this dark, evergreen tunnel, only a distant glimpse of the Pacific is visible; in the afternoon, when the sun is striking the water, this patch becomes a blinding flash of light. At the complex itself, a tower establishes the vertical anchor of the composition, and the clustered shacks gradually fall away to within just fifteen feet from where the coast drops off into the water.

Fixtures and decorations are kept to a minimum—only some venting pipes, skylights, ship's lamps, and strips of copper decorate the roof. Building materials are allowed to age naturally so that they blend into the landscape's gray and brown rocks and golden grasses: thick posts are connected to lintels with bolts and steel plates that have rusted to blend with the wood, flashing strips lining the walls and the roofs have tarnished to a coppery green, and planks are attached to the structures with metal nails that streak rust down the vertical grains of wood.

Ten condominiums are arranged around two internal courts, creating outdoor spaces

Georges Seurat
*A Sunday Afternoon on the Island of
La Grande Jatte.* 1884–86
Oil on canvas, 6'9" × 10' ⅜"
(205.5 × 305.8 cm)
Helen Birch Bartlett Memorial. The Art
Institute of Chicago

shielded from the relentless wind. The first courtyard is enclosed by dwellings for people and shelters for cars. A passageway leads to the second court, an inner sanctum arranged on a steep, grassy hill. Steps made of railroad ties and grassy treads casually wind down the hill, around a tree trunk, and to a torii that leads to the continental drop. The torii is simply framed by bare walls and a ceiling, making a gateway to the edge of the cliff and the distant blue horizon.

Another place where architecture is made to confront the sea in coastal conditions similar to California's is the rocky outcropping of Tanah Lot in Bali. The temple complex, built to appease the stormy gods of the South Seas, stands on a massive rock that is connected to the larger island by a low-lying sand flat, most of the time dotted with saltwater pools. Stairs carved directly into the stone wind up to the plateau, where an ensemble of umbrella pavilions surrounds a tall pagoda. The solidity of the rock contrasts with the delicate structures above, defying the moody sea. Ivy hangs over the monolithic rock, draping cavern entrances hollowed out over the centuries by crashing water. Sometimes, after a rise in the ocean tide, surf rushes over the sand to turn the mountain into an island, imbued with the mystery and power of isolation.

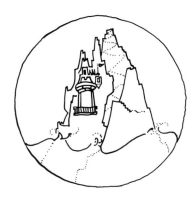

From the earliest written histories, islands have maintained a powerful hold on the imagination. They represent separation from the familiar world around us. The variety of islands around the world is extraordinary, ranging from the tiny Île de la Cité in Paris to continental Australia, from uninhabited islands deep in the Pacific to crowded Manhattan. Sometimes an island's isolation can foster unique forms of life, with appearances, habits, customs, and dispositions distinct from neighboring landmasses, as seen on Australia, the Galápagos, or Madagascar. People love to visit island retreats, but isolation and separation imposed by islands can be involuntary. When Prospero, the Shakespearean duke of Naples, is overthrown by his treacherous brother in *The Tempest*, he is exiled to an island and deprived of his rightful inheritance. Napoleon was vanquished by his island exile: in 1821 he died on Saint Helena, where he had been confined for six years. Islands sometimes signal a separation from legal and social norms, as is the case of the English schoolchildren who savagely hunt each other down in William Golding's *Lord of the Flies*.

The island that perhaps best symbolizes the power of legal and social norms is Alcatraz. Relying on the frigid isolation guaranteed by San Francisco harbor, the giant rock was once the site of one of the most feared prisons in the world.

Islands are not limited to the ocean. The Barcaccia Fountain in Rome is an island that sits in its own basin of water and has bridges for people to reach the drinking fountains. Rome's Tiber Island was a shrine to Asclepius, god of healing; hospitals were built on the river island long ago to take advantage of the natural quarantine against infectious diseases. The Phoenix Hall at the Byodo-in in Kyoto distinguishes the Buddha from worldly impurity by means of a lotus-filled lake. After seasonal rains, Lake Bratan in Bali surrounds a tiny island that is perfectly carpeted in dark green moss. When the rains stop, the lake dries, and the temple with eleven tiers becomes accessible by foot.

One of the most expressive fusions of island and architecture in the world is Mont-Saint-Michel, the monastic refuge rising out of the Atlantic off France's Normandy coast. The medieval compound merges so fundamentally with the island that the buildings seem to be carved from a monolithic mountain of stone. The island's earliest history dates from 708, when Aubert, bishop of Avranches, founded a monastery on the barren rock following a visitation by the Archangel Michael. Buildings were gradually piled on top of each other until the fourteenth century, when the crowning chapel (La Merveille) was finally completed. Near the bottom, houses cluster inside the wall. The collections of chimneys, gables, and dormers eventually reach the church foundations, whose heavy walls support the elongated gable of its roof. At the summit, a Gothic chapel, attached at an angle, rises out of the thick stone walls in a confident display of slender tracery and windows, with elaborate spires and grimacing gargoyles capping the pyramidal pile.

In the high towers, bells once chimed the hours governing the monastic routine, supplemented by the natural rhythms of the tides separating and linking the mountain in six-hour cycles that continue today. Cold salt water routinely spreads with impressive speed to the mountain's rocky base, where natural sea boulders fuse with the mortared stones of the walls, then retreats into its own depths, exposing the sand flats and connecting the island to the continent once again.

After touring the religious mountain, Henry Adams compiled his reactions in *Mont-Saint-Michel and Chartres*: "The Archangel loved heights. Standing on the summit of the tower that crowned his church, wings upspread, sword uplifted, the devil crawling beneath, and the cock, symbol of the eternal vigilance, perched on the mailed foot, Saint Michael held a place of his own in heaven and on earth. . . . So he stood for centuries on his Mount in Peril of the Sea, watching across the tremor of the immense ocean,—*immensi tremor oceani*,—as Louis XI, inspired for once to poetry, inscribed on the collar of the Order of Saint Michael which he created. So soldiers, nobles, and monarchs went on pilgrimage to his shrine; so the common people followed, and still follow, like ourselves."[67]

In the second century A.D., the Roman emperor Hadrian had an island built within his villa compound near Tivoli as a haven from the pressures of overseeing the burgeoning empire. On this marble island (named the Maritime Theater for mock naval skirmishes staged in the moat), the Roman ruler, builder, warrior, and statesman could entertain his special guests with lavish dinner parties. In *Rome and a Villa*, Eleanor Clark writes: "Hadrian is playing Robinson Crusoe, as everyone does in childhood and longs to do forever after; the island is the oldest, most necessary image, older than the Dying God; that is the true romantic impossible, to be separated from the rubs and nudges and impurities of society by the primordial, deathly medium of water."[68] Even though the moat was relatively narrow, it signaled that the island was off-limits, symbolically isolated from outside cares and concerns. All that is left of the island today is the band of water, marble column stumps, and fragments of the brick structures, but at one time it stood in the center of a vast mansion filled with both miniaturized buildings and monumental halls. Water was incorporated in the villa's rooms, atria, and gardens (presaging its sixteenth-century neighbor, the Villa d'Este) in pools luxuriously decorated in intricate mosaics, steaming caldaria, and secret water corridors.

Two thousand years later, another stone island was built, this time in Viscaya, Florida, for John Deering, who ruled over an empire of farm machinery manufacture. Designed in 1914 by F. Burral Hoffman as an elaborate breakwater in Biscayne Bay, the island sits within an elliptical inlet symmetrically carved into the coast, echoing the geometric themes of the formal gardens surrounding the main house. The island takes the shape of a proud marble ship (reminiscent of the Barcaccia in Rome or the stone junk in Beijing) run aground in the shallow water amid sand and rusticated stones. The boat is decorated with naval motifs of anchors and lines. Stairs on both port and starboard allow swimmers to board the stone deck. Spiky granite pylons shoot up from the marble balustrades lining the sides, where stone water gods and naked mermaids, carved by Alexander Stirling Calder (father of Alexander Calder), make up the barge's crew.

Tiny islands, not meant to be inhabited, create emotional tension through their partial or total inaccessibility. Being separated from the normal, even by the simplest ring of water, distinguishes them as potent places. The architect Victor Carrasco renovated some medieval fortifications for his home in Bornos, Spain, where a single lemon tree with a whitewashed trunk stands on a square island in the center of a pool. White walls surround a basin containing water that reflects light back through the opening above. The simple channel of water surrounding the tree distinguishes the island spatially from the rest of the house. The water acts as a frame for the tree, contrasting and highlighting every leaf, edge, and bit of light. Many tiny islands form a grid in the pool at the Oceanside Civic Center in California, which can also read as a grove since each island hosts a palm tree.

Tiny stepping-stone islands are most popular in Eastern gardens but are also used in the West. At the Heian Jingu shrine in Kyoto, a series of round stones form a path that allows visitors to walk out over the pond. The path is casually meandering, as if the islands had been placed randomly and by luck a negotiable path created. This practice is mimicked in the fountain in Lawrence Halprin's Levi Strauss Plaza in San Francisco, where stones guide the feet close to the waterfalls, combining a sense of danger with a feeling of isolation.

Oceans and islands create conditions of paradox. The infinity of the oceans magnifies the finite limits of the island. This principle plays a role in interpreting the incredible stone garden of Ryoan-ji in Kyoto, which, without a single drop of water, evokes the limitless ocean. A flat bed of raked white gravel portrays the ocean's flat surface, while fifteen stone islands are grouped in five clusters. Halos of green moss surround each island, separating the white stones from the white gravel. Around the peat-and-moss-covered lands, gardeners carefully rake the gravel in circular ripples that gradually merge with raked longitudinal bands striping the tray. A thin canal filled with larger chips surrounds the entire bed, separating the composition from the observer. Shadows thrown by the trees beyond the weathered walls come and go throughout the day but leave the stone garden unchanged. Like Hadrian's island or Mont-Saint-Michel, these islands are meant

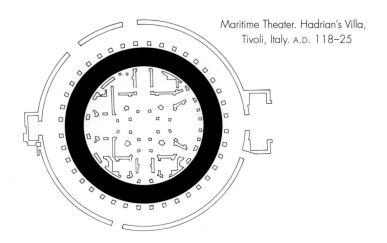

Maritime Theater. Hadrian's Villa, Tivoli, Italy. A.D. 118–25

to be physically and spiritually isolated. To step in the gravel would be tantamount to trespassing, with evidence recorded by footsteps disturbing the precise patterns.

A deck to one side provides a place to reflect on the garden's meaning. Are these pebbles and stones a metaphor for the sea, for the heavens, or the world? Or can they instead be a metaphor for life? Do they, like the Venetian marriage, allude to the mysterious and delicately tensioned union of the mortal and the immortal, finite and infinite, humankind and the sea?

Sandcastle, San Francisco, California

Opposite and overleaf: Mont-Saint-Michel, Normandy, France

Tanah Lot, Bali

Water temples, Lake Bratan, Ulu Danu, Bali

Lopez Island docks, San Juan Islands, Washington

Philipsburg, Saint Maarten, Dutch West Indies

Levi Strauss Plaza, San Francisco, California

Opposite: Heian Jingu, Kyoto, Japan

Oceanside Civic Center, California

Opposite: Carrasco House, Bornos, Spain

Tokyo Sea Life Park, Japan

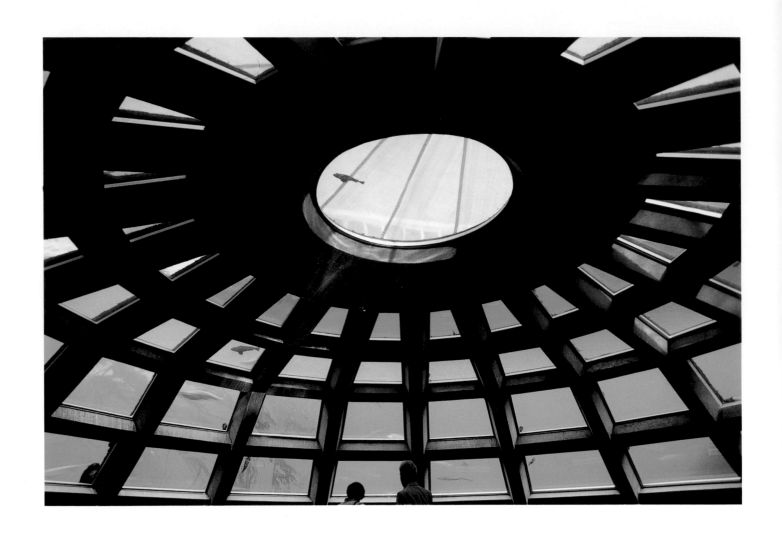

Seattle Aquarium, Washington

"Shark Experience," Marine World Africa U.S.A., Vallejo, California

Maritime Theater, Hadrian's Villa, Tivoli, Italy

Cultural Center Plaza, Kowloon, Hong Kong

Piazza San Marco, Venice, Italy

Hong Kong

Portofino, Italy

Port de Gustavia, Saint Barthélemy, French West Indies

Overleaf: Sea Ranch Condominium, Sea Ranch, California

Cruise ship, Caribbean

Opposite: Golden Gate Bridge, San Francisco, California

Torii Gate, near Miyajima Island, Japan

THE WATER OF ARCHITECTURE:
POTENTIAL FOR WONDER

n southwestern Pennsylvania, a vibrant stream called Bear Run storms down from forested Appalachian foothills, plunges in white foam over rocks and ancient boulders, sprays green ferns with fans of fractal leaves, and swirls into shallows soaking massive oak-tree roots. Midway in its course, the stream spills over a carbonaceous ledge in a sweeping cascade. Falling through the air, the water glazes and spins into white spider's silk, sinewy and striated, and then splashes down into a pool, tangling into froths, suds, and bubbles. Then, as the water pours over another ledge, it surges deeper into the forest, racing through an obstacle course of fallen logs, stones, and earthen dams.

It was to this compelling wilderness stream that Edgar and Liliane Kaufmann escaped from industrial Pittsburgh, where, during the 1920s, they owned the largest department store in town. For years the couple had retreated with their son Edgar to a small cottage they kept near the waterfall. When they decided to build a substantial house on the site in 1934, they commissioned a famous midwestern architect to design a house with a view of the stream and waterfall.

Frank Lloyd Wright understood the plight of Pittsburghers. The "nation's forge" was infamously known around the country as the "smoky city." Oppressive pollution choked immigrant slums, streetlamps had to burn at noon to penetrate the smog, and evenings were backlit by menacing orange auras from restless smelters. Virtually everything about the city offended Wright's ideals of "organic" architecture—of living in unison with the land, not dominating or controlling nature with reckless abandon. In fact, when frustrated city officials asked Wright how Pittsburgh could be saved, he replied, "It would be cheaper to destroy it."[69]

The house that Wright built for the Kaufmanns at Bear Run is a masterpiece of organic architecture. Named Fallingwater, the structure engages our senses of sight, sound, and touch, and compels us to see, hear, and feel not only the architecture but also nature beyond. Fusions, counterpoints, and tensions lead us to the *meaning* of the place—its connection to nature, its inhabitants, and the water.

Fallingwater is first a visual experience. Wright masterfully balances sweeping cantilevers against uplifting stone towers, smooth planes against textured stonework, transparent bands of windows against solid walls, and moving water against stationary architecture. With its cantilevers rigidly frozen in space high over the streambed, the structure seems to defy gravity. (When the Kaufmanns insisted Wright consult an engineer, he only grudgingly agreed. After the engineers confirmed the Kaufmanns' worst fears—that the maverick structure would collapse into the stream—Wright scoffed at the analyses and had the reports entombed in his unchanged foundations.) All through the house, Wright invited the forest in, using local, natural materials. Boulders emerge through the hearth, moss gardens grow under windows, and beams defer to trees, politely bending around their trunks. Masons constructed the tower that anchors into the boulders from indigenous stone, setting it in patterns to imitate the strains of stone ledges and rough oak-bark textures. Wright also opened the interior to the outside with walls of glass. Fieldstones paving the interior floors are coated with wax to simulate the water-glazed stones outside. Light reflected from the stream seems to dance on the ceilings, trees cast leafy shadows onto the walls, and muted sunlight infiltrates dark corridors through diffusing skylights.

Sound also permeates the house on every level, changing in rhythm and intensity throughout the cycle of Pennsylvania seasons. Among the head-high rhododendrons above the glen, before Fallingwater is visible, the concealed brook sends up audible signals that entice visitors into the forest. As one continues down the ravine path, the surge grows louder and louder, and the house suddenly comes into sight. At the entrance, a bridge spans water that quietly whirls before it is sent over a precipice ten yards away. Inside, when the windows are closed, the cascade's rush is kept to a low rumble. When the windows swing open, however, the full sound of the rapids invade the rooms. Collecting the runoff of melting snow, the waters of March storm loudly through the forest on their urgent downstream mission. Summer arrives and Bear Run swells to absorb generous June rains, sometimes flooding its banks but decelerating by August to a lethargic pace. The stream rests in autumn, when it clogs with fallen leaves and twigs, accompanied by wind rustling dry branches overhead. Not until deep winter does the water freeze into icy stalactites, silently resting until springtime.

The sense of touch is another essential aspect of Fallingwater. At the entry, a font catching a thin jet welcomes visitors; as in a church or a mosque, it is a place to wash before crossing the threshold. To the left, a pool with stone steps extends under the house. Trails wander up to the guesthouse, where a swimming pool collects springwater, or down to the cascade for an outdoor shower. The cascades throw mist and spray up to the decks, where people can "mentally lean out over" and psychologically connect with the stream, a dangerous thirty-foot drop below. Inside, Wright designed a staircase with a glass canopy that descends through an opening in the living-room floor. It is the umbilical cord that ties the water with the architecture. Suspended from metal strips, the steps lead directly into the stream's path, where the last platform hovers only inches above the surface, connecting people to the water constantly gliding by on its natural course.

In an age where water has become increasingly domesticated and decreasingly appreciated, even a short visit to Bear Run is filled with affirmations of water's indefatigable magic and excitement. The messages are especially potent since many of us have grown accustomed to taking fresh, clean water for granted. Water instantly flows out of our kitchen faucets (or dishwashers, hot-water heaters, toilets, lawn sprinklers, Jacuzzis, showers, and ice-cube makers), and most of us give little thought to where the water came from or where it goes after we pull the plug. Modern treatment plants have replaced the natural water cycle with a mechanized hydrologic cycle of collection, filtration, and sedimentation. After the water passes standardized purity tests, it is released into networks of underground pipes and, with the turn of a wrist, fills our waiting glasses.

All of this effort is expended for the simple reason that we need water to live. Undeniably, water has a tangible physical hold on the lives of every one of us. But, as we have seen, water also has many intangible meanings for humans, ranging from birth in the amniotic fluid to death in the mythical waters of the river Styx. More than anything, designs involving water and architecture must remind people of this dual impact that water has on our lives.

The reminders can be very simple. In ancient Pompeii was a drinking fountain for people and donkeys. It had a straightforward shape and made water conveniently available for the townspeople and their animals. Above the fountain was a relief depicting a cloud with a rain god on top. For the donkeys, the relief added nothing of value to the water, but for the women and men who came there to drink, it was a reminder of where the water had come from and how it fit into their religious and physical scheme of the world. The relief invested the fountain with meaning, communicating something about Pompeian beliefs and attitudes and reminding that people are not donkeys.

Architects use materials and forms to communicate ideas. When we make places that include water in our designs, we cannot ignore the role that history and symbolism play in fortifying connections among people, water, and nature. Perhaps the greatest lesson of our century has been that people need connections to the past, and myths or religions, to help make some sense of our increasingly complex world. If architecture were merely built of materials and composed of empty forms, then fountains, gardens, or buildings would mean nothing more to people than did the Pompeii fountain for the donkeys drinking there. Clearly this is not the case. In reality, materials (stone, plants, or water, for example) and forms (arches, statues, gardens, or pools) are rich with shared or personal meanings. From the ordering of materials and forms the observer should be able to understand something about the use of the design and something about the people by and for whom it was built.

Wayward turtles, sunken barges, flinching river gods, and winged sea horses invest the Roman fountains—Tartarughe, Barcaccia, Four Rivers, and the Trevi—with a resoundingly human dimension. Their lesson is that people know and love places not only for physical attributes, but also for the colorful tales and legends passed on from generation to generation. What would the water in Venice be without its tradition, or the river in Paris without its history? Stourhead not only reminds us of the ideal people once placed in emulating nature in pursuit of beauty, but also allows us to step out of our lackluster shoes and step into the shoes of Aeneas, a great hero from the past. A similar kind of reverence and enthusiasm for nature invests Japanese and Chinese gardens with a palpable spirit, so that every stone, every plant, and every body of water embodies a particular ideal of nature accessible to those patient enough to seek it out.

Water is a natural material with an unchanging identity, wherever it appears in architecture or nature, whether in Kyoto, Fort Worth, Amsterdam, or Sebatu, Bali. Its use in architecture should reflect the attitude about the natural world held by the people who design, construct, or inhabit the building. Since our own relation to the natural world has superseded the historic Western imposition of a geometric order on nature or the Eastern quest for "naturalness," our use of water in architectural composition will be related to the more complex geometries of our own day, which operate in time as well as in space. At the end of our millennium, we are faced with the dilemma of balancing human needs with respect for nature. If water is being used neither much nor well in our own architecture, then surely some of the difficulty can be traced to our confusion over what sort of attitude toward nature we are trying to express. Yet if we can effectively incorporate water's symbolism, history, and physical nature, then our water and architecture can have a potential for wonder unmatched by any other material that we can include in our environments.

Architecture and water engage us by letting us see, hear, and touch the water in a myriad of ways. Sight, sound, and contact characterized the inception of all the places we have seen—from medieval Chinese gardens to European canal cities to harbors old and new. Architecture is an intermediary that negotiates connections or separations between people and water, communicating sensory clues through forms and materials. But what combination of senses make places successful, so that fountains, pools, rivers, harbors, gardens, islands, or streams inspire, amuse, rescue, frighten, or challenge us? What similar clues lead us to understand a city's history, a fountain's meaning, or a garden's spirit?

Designers at Giverny, Katsura, San Antonio, and even the Piazza di Spagna in Rome, use reflection, dance, and stillness to create places where people can escape the ordinary, relieve tired minds, or block out distractions. The success of Monet's pond derives from its surface, which is literally filled with reflection. Gardeners engulfed the banks with irises, flooded the surface with lilies, and created a canopy of branches and vines, all fusing to make Giverny an Edenic microenvironment. Katsura's success depends on landscaping devices that build up the shores with rich counterpoints of shapes, colors, and textures to achieve a sense of closure. San Antonio's secret is that the waterway is separated from the city by a winding canyon (we never see it entirely but have to follow its unfolding course) lined with inviting restaurants, friendly shops, and intimate theaters. The River Walk disconnects us from the rest of the city and draws us together along an interactive street. Like nearly all fountains, the Barcaccia casts spells on people by its magical manipulation of water. Through a sleight of hand, spewing shells, squirting jets, and water sloshing over the decks divert attention away from crazed motorists reeling through the piazza.

Designers also use the qualities of reflection, depth, or the seemingly infinite surface of large bodies of water to relieve claustrophobia and expand personal space. Instead of hypnotically drawing us inward, the waters of the Four Rivers Fountain, Shugaku-in, Stourhead, Lower Slaughter, and the garden of the Master of the Nets release our spirits, guiding our eyes into the sky, the mesmerizing depths of a pool, or spacious landscapes. The charming liquid choreography of the Four Rivers Fountain and the mountain's obelisk-capped ascent lift spirits upward and out of the crowded city. Water at Stourhead helps to deepen space by pulling the foreground forward and pushing the background back. The pond's edges, so carefully integrated into the landscape, undulate to lengthen the perimeter and make the surface area seem larger than if it were a simple circle or oval. Unlike Giverny's edges, which crowd out views into the French countryside, Shugaku-in incorporates neighboring mountains (always an image of wide open space) and rice fields into its design, so that the garden communicates with the "authentic" and expansive landscape beyond. If the stream flowing through Lower Slaughter were an asphalt lane, it would undoubtedly lose its magic: asphalt lanes do not call to mind all asphalt lanes in the world. As a connecting waterway, however, its currents carry the imagination beyond the town, through central England, to the infinite ocean. On the other hand, the Master of the Nets, with its liquid courtyard, relieves claustrophobia by creating a negative space that in the middle of crowded Suzhou is refreshingly empty.

Like Suzhou, jam-packed Hong Kong constantly barrages the mind with noises and restless commotion, but along its long edge, the harbor contrasts the city's hyperdensity with a wide open field of blue that, in spite of ships and boats, grants us a freeing vision of releasing emptiness. A substantial part of the wonder of the Sea Ranch condominiums is that embracing courtyards and sheltering interiors break loose through openings, passageways, or windows to the vast expanse of the Pacific. People can choose, according to their needs or moods, to be in a small, intimate space or to stand at the edge of the cliff and connect emotionally with the sea. For scientists cooped up in small laboratories, the court at the Salk Institute must be a welcoming relief. Tired eyes can follow Louis Kahn's narrow channel as it becomes thinner and thinner in perspective until it falls into Shelley's "unfathomable sea."

Channels of water are excellent devices for unifying complicated architectural arrangements. Waterways can link a series of incidents or provide an element of continuity within a city, such as Chicago, where skyscrapers (a forest of Wrigleys, Tribunes, Monadnocks, and Searses) contrast with the unchanging river and lakeshore. When gardeners release the valves at the Villa d'Este, water races through the fountains like the ball bearings in Japanese Pachinko games and, through its constant downward rush, weaves the garden together. At the Villa Lante, Vignola ingeniously used a liquid spine for his symmetrical arrangement of Renaissance balance and harmony. At both the Villa d'Este and the Villa Lante, we can perceive (though not quite see) the continuous flow of water through several chapters of an unfolding saga. In the same vein but on a grander scale, the Nile's water acted as the main transportation artery, the source (during its flooding) of essential nutrients, and a symbol of Egypt. Parisians do not rely on the Seine to flood Notre Dame or the Latin Quarter, nor is it much used for transportation anymore, but it continues to link monuments, parks, bridges, and streets into a coherent city and absorb the reflections of the buildings lined up along its banks.

There is something about reflection that stirs the heart. Reflection should be used sparingly when dignifying important buildings, but it can be used generously to make ordinary buildings seem more pleasing. Not every building can (or ought to) be lavished with costly materials, but reflecting water can give a building a little extra something. Even though the majority of vernacular buildings in Venice, Suzhou, and Amsterdam are humble, the reflecting water in the canals fills them with a magic that the same type of buildings in drier cities cannot match. Reflective water adds an element of fantasy to architecture by filling shadows with reflected light, transforming the solidity of stone or brick to shifting water and painting what would otherwise be a gray asphalt road with constantly changing color.

People marvel at reflections: Narcissus adored his own image in the water, and visitors to the lavishly carved and gilded Byodo-in and Kinkaku-ji contemplate visions of the treasured object as a heavenly mansion. If the reflecting pool at the Taj Mahal were drained and planted with grass, the tomb would lose a great deal of its mystery. Reflective water idealizes places we build to symbolize the gods we worship, the heroes we intend to remember, or the ideals we cherish. Moreover, the pools clear out an unoccupiable space in front of buildings so that we can view them free of more mundane components of a city. The water in the Tidal Basin and the Reflecting Pool signals that the Jefferson, Lincoln, and Washington monuments are very special and are distinguished from the other monuments, agencies, and landmarks in Washington, D.C.

Architects can use the flat plane that water naturally seeks as an embellishment for compositions. Like the Egyptian pyramids standing in their sea of sand or the Statue of Liberty rising out of New York harbor, Mont-Saint-Michel is a potent three-dimensional object in its own right, but the two-dimensional sheet of water that surrounds it episodically magnifies the outline and sculptural quality of the stirring image. The magic of the Piazza San Marco in Venice is due in part to the pavement extending uninterrupted into the flat lagoon as well as the apparent flatness of its surface, which helped to earn its distinction as the "drawing room" of Europe. (We are tricked into thinking the piazza itself is perfectly flat by the linear paving pattern, which establishes the horizontal plane strongly enough so that the darker pavement between the lines can slope unobserved to the drains.) In addition to the symbolic notion of tying the most important urban space with the sea, a more physical reality is ushered in when high tide invades and floods the piazza, in minutes creating a lagoon among the buildings. If the Torii threshold were moved to the center of a city or transplanted to a garden, it would lose virtually all of its mystique. The flat blue plane of the bay sets the image apart, contrasting the gate with a field of changing color and isolating it from physical approach, forcing us to pass through in our imaginations or occasionally in boats. In the same sense, we cannot get close enough to touch the mythological menagerie in the Trevi but must use our imaginations to cross the broad, liquid proscenium and connect with the sprays and sounds of the Acqua Vergine streaming from Oceanus.

Like the purely visual aspects of water, the sounds of water are variable and can be manipulated to produce satisfying results. Water makes sound as it splashes against things, moves over solid objects, or falls into itself. Attention to the audible aspects of water is important—too little sound can be annoying (like a dripping faucet), and too much sound in confined spaces (like shopping malls) can be overpowering and trite. Franz Liszt spent time at an apartment in the Villa d'Este and was influenced by the sounds of the fountains when he composed "Les Jeux à la Villa d'Este." In "La Mer," Claude Debussy tried to simulate the sounds of the sea, violently stormy in full chords or gently lapping in soft dissonances and consonances. Like his contemporary in Venice, the painter Canaletto, George Frederick Handel was inspired by the pageantry of water festivals, fireworks, and royal processions on the Thames. And Vivaldi described scenes from the four seasons through the *pizzicato* of raindrops, the apprehensive, swaying rhythm of an impending summer storm, and its gusty release, *con spirito*.

Designs can borrow from natural cycles and sounds already present: Fallingwater is constantly filled with the seasonal stream sounds, as Mont-Saint-Michel and the Sea Ranch are always surrounded by the sounds of the sea. But in the absence of brooks or oceans, designers can use water to simulate sounds that allow people to connect with nature, refresh spent minds, or block out less desirable noises. The Lovejoy in Oregon is an unexpected surprise in the center of tame Portland for its impressive amount of water seemingly gone out of control. Cascade Charley at the University of Oregon, designed by Alice Wingwall, is a much sought after neighbor at lunchtime for the lively sound of its waters.

Silence, too, is appreciated. Water often makes no sound at all, or very little, so people find emotional rescue in the rare commodity of silence. Just the right amount of water noise can take the edge off of silence, producing "white noise." In the middle of Rome, the Tartarughe Fountain only drips feeble squirts of water but is somehow just loud enough to spark the imagination. At the Alhambra, the fountains are relatively quiet, but the stone cloisters, walls, columns, and pavements create enchanting echoes and reverberations of the trickles. Lakes are particularly quiet, drawing people to connect with their stillness, or, like Goethe and Thoreau, to commune with the "indwelling spirit," and the Ryoan-ji garden uses stones to create a world that is utterly soundless.

Water touching our skin is the most personally intimate experience we can have of it. Degrees of contact range from being misted by warm steam sprays in San Antonio's HemisFair Park, or being splashed by the waterfall walkway in downtown Seattle, to being completely immersed in the Sebatu bathing pits or the caldaria of Bath. Immersion is a kind of escape, a form of disconnection from the world above the surface. John Cheever wrote about a troubled man who tried to escape the disappointments of life by swimming across his stuffy New England suburb, swimming pool by swimming pool. Contact with water can signal entrance into prayerful composure: Muslims wash their feet and hands before entering a mosque, and some Christians dab a bit of "holy" water on their forehead upon entering a church. There is also something about contact with water that frees our inhibitions and spirits, just as it did for Gene Kelly in *Singin' in the Rain* or Fellini's cinematic Venus in the Trevi Fountain in *La Dolce Vita*.

Water meant for contact should, through its architecture, send out messages of invitation. It is essential that a fountain's pipes, lights, and wires be safely concealed. Nothing is worse than to see the mechanical innards of a fountain or pool, especially when the water is turned off in cold seasons or dry spells. Water should seem *alive*, so that people do not feel as if they are standing in a limp shower or swimming in a stagnant pool. The pools at Sebatu are always kept in motion so that they charge the water with vitality and freshness. The upsurging jets in the Fountain Place in Dallas are liquid beacons for people to approach, challenge the water, and sacrifice their dryness.

To invite contact, still water must seem fresh, clear, sparkling, and clean—full of messages of beauty and health. An effective way to achieve this is to fill the water with dancing color. Outdoor pools meant for swimming should be exposed to and warmed by the sun. Ricardo Legorreta uses solid planes of vibrant color to make the water seem especially pure, a trick used by Arquitectonica and Victor Carrasco with similar success. Pools, like the ones in Maui, can shimmer in the sun and be dramatically illuminated at night so that the colors, patterns, steps, or reflections pulsate as if the water were alive, inviting people to descend.

In *Rome and a Villa*, Eleanor Clark writes about the Trevi Fountain: "This is the last, royal chamber of the dream; the immersion is complete, more obviously so from the basin's being below street level like the boat in Piazza di Spagna; the stepping down is part of the imaginative process, like the descent into wells and pools in fairy tales, after which you feel no serious distinction of kind between the ocean characters of the fountains and the promenade hour swarms. . . . The piazza is engulfed."[70] If the Barcaccia and the Trevi were lifted above people's downward gazes and onto a podium, they would lose their qualities of separation from normal life in the streets. Descent heightens our removal from the world at large. A considerable part of the magic in Paris and San Antonio is that people can move below the street level of the city to the plane of the river, heightening the feeling of escape and disconnection. Similarly, visitors at the Tokyo Sea Life Park descend from the surface above to the underwater spectacle, and the grotto at Stourhead brings us closer to the mystery of the water source.

While contact with water is an essential and popular aspect of many designs, in some places physical contact has little to do with its spirit. These days, vigilant guards turn away fountain jumpers who come to the Trevi expecting a swim. Few people would consider the idea of swimming in Monet's pond or the pools at the Humble Administrator's Garden—their still waters (not quite stagnant, but murky) do not convey a sense of being fit for swimming that the waters in Sebatu, the Pink House, or Hearst's Neptune pool convey. Splashing around the pensive reflecting pools at the Lincoln Memorial, the Taj Mahal, or the Brion Cemetery would disrupt their serene dignity and blaspheme their sacred intentions, just as skinny-dipping at Stourhead would disturb its tranquillity.

Emotional contact with water occurs when people are allowed to get as close as possible without actually touching it, resulting in our famous "mental leaning out over." The most important thing to consider when making designs involving emotional contact with water is the edge. San Antonio is one of the most exemplary cases of communicative contact with a river. Even though the river is sunken in a winding corridor, people can walk along its sidewalks and cross on its low bridges. Often the river is only a few steps away; there may be no railings at all, with only a curb marking the distinction between land and water. The Fort Worth Water Gardens would not be as delightful if people were prevented from getting close to the water. Handrails and barriers would make it seem too safe. Visitors may choose to safely watch from above as the water rushes into the pit, or from below as it rushes down at them.

From Paris to Tokyo to Fort Worth, every drop of water on the planet takes part in the water cycle. The cycle guarantees that all water is connected in a continuous global chain, so that water never remains an isolated incident and never exclusively belongs to any specific time or place. Even the tiniest drop of water shares a heritage with the greatest ocean. If we could trace water's movement (like biologists do with radio-tagged elk in Yellowstone or tigers in Bengal), we might see water pooling in Kyoto reappear in Hong Kong harbor, or water gushing from the Trevi Fountain resurface at the Villa d'Este.

The spirit of the Trevi is a celebration of the entire water cycle, personified by Oceanus, who commands the release, distribution, collection, and evaporation of the Earth's water. In the words of its architect, Nicola Salvi, the fountain "shows the essential mobility of water, which never ceases in its operation and is incapable of ever remaining still, even for the briefest moment."[71] In Kyoto, the image of the bamboo fountain represents the arrival of water from the vast bodies of water circulating beyond the small garden. "Eternity consists of opposites," Seneca wrote; to understand the oceanic infinities is to appreciate the finite flume. This is equally true for Kahn's Salk Institute plaza, where the thin vein evokes the inevitable return of water to the oceanic receptacle. The Neptune pool at San Simeon is stirring because we see that, although it is enormous, when compared to the ocean it represents only a minute drop. The Ryoan-ji stone garden performs the greatest feat by making us think of water when we only see stones. Contained in the rectangular plot is a profoundly simple view of the ocean, perfectly balanced, perfectly harmonious.

Finally, we return to Sen no Rikyū's legendary tea garden. Inside its hedge, visitors would have heard the subliminal murmurs of an unseen sea. In the stone font, people would have dipped their hands in the water, perhaps seeing their own reflection rippling across the tiny mirror. Comparing the few cups of water with the limited view of the sea invested the garden with a subtle but resounding message—that every drop of water in the world is connected with all the rest. It was a masterful combination of the senses. Through the careful arrangement of water and architecture, we can create for ourselves a place in the nature surrounding us—a place like Fallingwater, the Hearst pool, the Salk Institute, the Kyoto basins, or the Trevi—connected to the cycle, and all of the world's water.

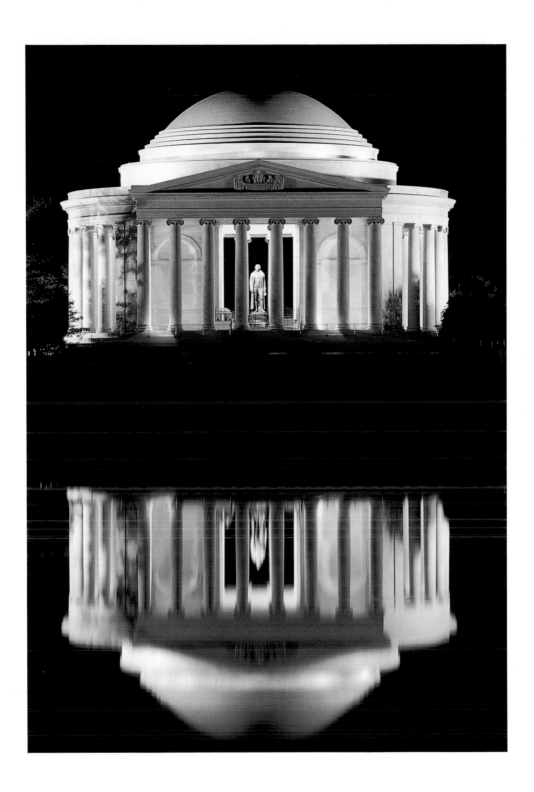

Jefferson Memorial, Washington, D.C.

Overleaf: Customs House and Santa Maria della Salute, Venice

Grand Wailea Resort, Maui, Hawaii

Zhouzheng Yuan, Suzhou, China

Opposite: Bang Pa-in, Thailand

Roman Bath, Bath, England

Opposite: The Mirage, Las Vegas, Nevada

Overleaf: Tokyo Sea Life Park, Japan

NOTES

1. Loraine E. Kuck, *The Art of Japanese Gardens* (New York: The John Day Company, 1940), 150.

2. Muriel Rukeyser, "The Speed of Darkness," in *The Speed of Darkness* (New York: Random House, 1968), 111.

3. Marcus Aurelius, *Meditations*, trans. A. S. L. Farquharson (Oxford: Oxford University Press, 1989), 31.

4. John 4:14, in *The New Oxford Annotated Bible*, ed. Bruce M. Metzger and Roland E. Murphy (Oxford: Oxford University Press, 1991), 129.

5. Lao-tzu, *Tao Te Ching*, trans. Stephen Mitchell (New York: Harper and Row Publishers, 1988), verse 8.

6. *The Qur'an, The First American Version*, trans. T. B. Irving (Brattleboro: Amana Books, 1985), 172.

7. Kuo-hsi, *An Essay on Landscape Painting*, trans. Shio Sakanishi (London: John Murray, 1959), 47–48.

8. John Keats, *Life, Letters, and Literary Remains of John Keats*, intro. Robert Lynd (London: J. M. Dent and Sons, 1959), xv.

9. Thomas Stearns Eliot, "Little Gidding, Four Quartets," in *The Complete Poems and Plays 1909–1950* (New York: Harcourt, Brace, and Company, 1952), 140.

10. Leonardo da Vinci, *The Notebooks*, trans. Edward MacCurdy (New York: Reynal and Hitchcock, 1938), 12.

11. Frederik Paludan-Müller, *The Fountain of Youth*, trans. Humphrey William Freeland (Philadelphia: Lippincott, 1867), 31–32.

12. William Blake, "The Marriage of Heaven and Hell," in *The Poetry and Prose of William Blake*, ed. David V. Erdman (New York: Doubleday and Company, 1965), 36.

13. William Shakespeare, *Hamlet*, in *Complete Works of William Shakespeare* (New York: Avenel Books, 1975), 1076.

14. Eliot, "Gerontion", in *Complete Poems and Plays 1909–1950*, 21.

15. Sir James George Frazer, *The Golden Bough, A Study in Magic and Religion* (New York: Avenel Books, 1923), 62.

16. D. H. Lawrence, *Women in Love* (New York: Penguin Books, 1981), 306.

17. Sextus Julius Frontinus, "Aqueducts of Rome," in *Aqueducts and Stratagems of Rome*, trans. Charles E. Bennett (New York: William Heinemann, 1925), sec. 10, 350.

18. Ezekiel 36:25, in *The New Oxford Annotated Bible*, 1106–7.

19. Mircea Eliade, *The Sacred and the Profane, The Nature of Religion*, trans. Willard R. Trask (New York: Harvest / Harcourt, Brace, Jovanovich, 1959), 130.

20. Hereward Lester Cooke, Jr., "The Documents Relating to the Fountain of Trevi," *Art Bulletin* 38, no. 3: 169, quotes Filarete in Bibl. Vat. MS 8235, 1762, who is quoting Nicola Salvi verbatim.

21. Genesis 2:10, in *The New Oxford Annotated Bible*, 4.

22. Henry Wadsworth Longfellow, "Evangeline," in *Voices of the Night, Ballads and Other Poems by Henry Wadsworth Longfellow* (New York: H. M. Caldwell, 1904), 82.

23. Antonio Averlino, Il Filarete, "Treatise on Architecture," in *Literary Sources of Art History*, ed. Elizabeth Gilmore Holt (Princeton: Princeton University Press, 1947), 145–46.

24. Lao-tzu, *Tao Te Ching*, verse 78.

25. Plato, *Phaedo*, in *The Dialogues of Plato*, trans. R. S. Bluck (New York: Bantam Books, 1986), 126–27.

26. Aristotle, *Meterologica*, trans. H. D. P. Lee (Cambridge: Harvard University Press, The Loeb Classical Library, 1987), 139–41.

27. Athanasius Kircher, *Mundus Subterraneus* (Weyerstraten: Amselodami, Apud Joannem Janssonium & Elizeum, 1665).

28. Ernest Brehaut, *An Encyclopedist of the Dark Ages, Isidore of Seville* (New York: Burt Franklin, 1912), 241.

29. Paul A. Underwood, "The Fountain of Life in Manuscripts of the Gospels," *Dumbarton Oaks Papers*, no. 5 (1950): 106.

30. Salomon de Caus, *New and Rare Inventions in Water Works* (London: printed by Joseph Moxon, 1659).

31. Bernard Forest de Belidor, *Architecture Hydraulique* 4 (Paris: Rue St. Jacques, Chez Charles Antoine Jombert, 1739).

32. Richard Wilbur, "Piazza di Spagna, Early Morning," in *A Roman Collection, Stories, Poems, and Other Good Pieces by the Writing Residents of the American Academy in Rome*, ed. Miller Williams (Columbia: University of Missouri Press, 1980), 67.

33. Cooke, "The Documents Relating to the Fountain of Trevi," 169.

34. Alberti is quoted in Marie Louise Gothein, *A History of Garden Art*, trans. Mrs. Archer-Hind (London and Toronto, 1928), 1, p. 273.

35. Langston Hughes, "The Negro Speaks of Rivers," in *The Weary Blues* (New York: Alfred A. Knopf, 1926), 51.

36. Heraclitus, *On the Universe*, trans. W. H. S. Jones (Cambridge: Harvard University Press, The Loeb Classical Library, 1959), 483.

37. Edgar Allan Poe, *The Complete Tales and Poems of Edgar Allan Poe* (New York: Vintage Books, 1975), 612–13.

38. Lewis Mumford, *The City in History* (New York: Harcourt, Brace, and World, 1961), 71.

39. Samuel Noah Kramer, ed., *Mythologies of the Ancient World* (Chicago: Quadrangle Books, 1961), 122.

40. Herodotus, *The History*, trans. David Grene (Chicago: University of Chicago Press, 1987), 138.

41. Marcus Vitruvius Pollio, *Ten Books of Architecture,* trans. Frank Granger (Cambridge: Harvard University Press, 1970), 8, pp. 135–36.

42. Mark Twain, *Life on the Mississippi* (New York: Viking Penguin Books, 1984), 201.

43. Eliot, "The Dry Salvages," in *Complete Poems and Plays 1909–1950*, 130.

44. Green Payton, *San Antonio: City in the Sun* (New York: McGraw-Hill, 1946), 194.

45. Leon Battista Alberti, *On the Art of Building*, trans. Joseph Rykwert, Neil Leach, and Robert Travernor (Cambridge: MIT Press, 1988), 109.

46. C. S. Lewis, *Out of the Silent Planet* (London: The Bodley Head, 1959), 71.

47. Italo Calvino, *Invisible Cities*, trans. William Weaver (New York: Harcourt, Brace, Jovanovich, 1972), 15, 86, 90.

48. Thomas Mann, *Death in Venice* (New York: Vintage International, 1989), 19.

49. Marco Polo, *The Travels of Marco Polo*, trans. Ronald Latham (New York: Penguin Books, 1958), 212.

50. Louis I. Kahn, *What Will Be Has Always Been, The Words of Louis Kahn*, ed. Richard Saul Wurnman (New York: Rizzoli, 1986), 216.

51. Metropolitan Museum of Art, *Monet's Years at Giverny: Beyond Impressionism* (New York: Harry N. Abrams, Inc., 1978), 28.

52. Gaston Bachelard, *Water and Dreams, An Essay on the Imagination of Matter* (Dallas: Pegasus Foundation, 1983), 28.

53. Richard Wigmore, *Schubert: The Complete Song Texts* (London: Victor Gollancz, 1988), 57.

54. Virgil quoted in Gilbert Highet, *Poets in a Landscape* (New York: Alfred A. Knopf, 1957), 146.

55. Henry David Thoreau, *Walden* (Boston: Ticknor & Fields, 1865), 191.

56. Teng Ch'ien quoted in Osvald Siren, *The Chinese on the Art of Painting* (New York: Schocken Books, 1963), 89.

57. Kuck, *The Art of Japanese Gardens*, 28.

58. Carl Jung, *Memories, Dreams, and Reflections*, ed. Aniela Jaffe, trans. Richard and Clara Winston (New York: Pantheon Books, 1973), 6–7.

59. Thomas Whately, *Observations on Modern Gardening*, ed. John Dixon Hunt (London: Garland Publishing, 1982), 61.

60. H. Paul Caemmerer, *The Life of Pierre-Charles L'Enfant: Planner of the City Beautiful the City of Washington* (Washington, D.C.: National Republic Publishing Co., 1950), 153.

61. Alvise Zorzi, *Venice, The Golden Age* (New York: Abbeville Press, 1983), 24.

62. Percy Bysshe Shelley, "Unfathomable Sea," in *The Eternal Sea, An Anthology of Sea Poetry*, ed. W. M. Williamson (Freeport: Books for Libraries Press, 1946), 160.

63. Jules Verne, *Twenty Thousand Leagues Under the Sea* (Los Angeles: Plantin Press, 1956), 74.

64. Thomas King, *Water. Miracle of Nature* (New York: Macmillan, 1953), 49.

65. Herman Melville, *Moby Dick, or the Whale* (New York: Russell and Russell, n.d.), 2.

66. Gordon Cullen, "Immediacy," *Architectural Review* 113 (April 1953): 236.

67. Henry Adams, *Mont-Saint-Michel and Chartres* (New York: Penguin Classics, 1986), 7.

68. Eleanor Clark, *Rome and a Villa* (Garden City: Doubleday and Company, 1952), 180.

69. *The Master Architect, Conversations with Frank Lloyd Wright*, ed. Patrick J. Meehan (New York: John Wiley and Sons, 1984), 8.

70. Clark, *Rome and a Villa*, 65.

71. Cooke, "The Documents Relating to the Fountain of Trevi."

LIST OF COLOR PHOTOGRAPHS

The authors and publisher would like to thank the institutions and private owners who provided access for photography. Numbers preceding the entries refer to page numbers.

1: Victor Carrasco. Private home built within late medieval fortifications with modern renovations, Bornos, Spain. 1989–90

2: Ricardo Legorreta. Solana: a joint venture of Maguire Thomas Partners and IBM. Westlake, Texas. 1986

4: Roger Deweese Inc. & Associates (fountain); WZMH Group California, Inc. (building). Wateridge Marketing Pavilion, San Diego, California. Completed 1983

8–9: Philibert de l'Orme and Jean Bullant. Château de Chenonceaux, spanning the river Cher, France. Begun 1513

11: Niki de Saint-Phalle and Jean Tinguely. Rites of Spring Fountain: *Love (The Lips),* Place Igor-Stravinsky, Paris, France. 1983

12–13: Nicola Salvi. Trevi Fountain, Rome, Italy. 1732–62

14: Bamboo Fountain, Byodo-in, Kyoto, Japan. 1053

24–25: Nicola Salvi. Trevi Fountain, Rome, Italy. 1732–62

26–27: Venice, Italy

28: Lighthouse, San Giorgio, Venice, Italy

29: Ricardo Legorreta. Solana Marriott. Solana: a joint venture of Maguire Thomas Partners and IBM. Westlake, Texas. 1986

30–31: Saiho-ji, Kyoto, Japan. Begun 8th century

32: I. M. Pei. Bank of China, Hong Kong. 1990 (Fountain consultant: R. J. Van Seters Co.)

33: Attributed to Giacomo da Vignola. Villa Lante, Bagnaia, Italy. Begun 1566

34: Philip Johnson. Fort Worth Water Gardens, Texas. 1975

35: Ryoan-ji, Kyoto, Japan. As early as 1488

36–37: Philip Johnson. Fort Worth Water Gardens, Texas. 1975

50: Ritual baths, Sebatu, Bali

51–52: Pirro Ligorio. Avenue of the One Hundred Fountains, Villa d'Este, Tivoli, Italy. Begun 1550

53: Attributed to Girolamo Rainaldi. Farnese Fountain, resting in ancient granite tubs from the Baths of Caracalla, Piazza Farnese, Rome, Italy. c. 1627

54: Saint Francis Woods, San Francisco, California

55: Attributed to Taddeo di Leonardo Landini. Tartarughe Fountain, Piazza Mattei, Rome, Italy. 1581–84

56–57: Anibal Gonzalez. Plaza de España, Seville, Spain. Built for the 1929 Ibero-American Exposition

58: Gianlorenzo Bernini. Fountain of the Four Rivers, Piazza Navona, Rome, Italy. 1647–51

59: Attributed to Giacomo della Porta, rebuilt by Gianlorenzo Bernini. Il Moro Fountain, Piazza Navona, Rome, Italy. 1575

60: Attributed to Pietro Bernini. Barcaccia Fountain, Piazza di Spagna, Rome, Italy. 1627

61: Fountain of Joy, Piazza del Campo, Siena, Italy. Original designer Jacopo della Quercia, 15th century; reproduction by Tito Sarrocchi, 1868

62–63: Pirro Ligorio. Villa d'Este, Tivoli, Italy. Begun 1550

64: Waterfalls at L'Esposizione Universale di Roma (EUR), Rome, Italy. Designed 1937, built 1950s

65: Generalife, Granada, Spain. Begun early 14th century

66: Howard Fields & Associates and SWA Group. Hyatt Regency Scottsdale at Gainey Ranch, Scottsdale, Arizona. 1987

67: Ford, Powell & Carson. HemisFair Park, San Antonio, Texas. 1968

68–69: Dan Kiley, Peter Kerr Walker, and WET Design. Fountain Place, Dallas, Texas. 1986

70: Paul Manship. *Prometheus.* Rockefeller Center, New York City. 1934. Water jets are a modern addition.

71: Jean Tinguely and Niki de Saint-Phalle. Rites of Spring Fountain: *The Firebird,* Place Igor-Stravinsky, Paris, France. 1983

72–73: Philip Johnson. Fort Worth Water Gardens, Texas. 1975

74–75: Precious Belt Bridge, Suzhou, China. 9th century

86–87: Venice, Italy

88–89: Robert H. H. Hugman and The River Beautification Project. River Walk, San Antonio, Texas. Begun 1938

90: Lu Zhi, China

91–93: Suzhou, China

94: Bruges, Belgium

95: Lower Slaughter, Wiltshire, England

96–97: Anibal Gonzalez. Plaza de España, Seville, Spain. Built for the 1929 Ibero-American Exposition

98–99: Attributed to Taddeo Gaddi or Neri di Fioravante. Ponte Vecchio, Florence, Italy. Mid-14th century reconstruction

100: Robert Adam. Pulteney Bridge, Bath, England. 1769–74

101: Richard Jones. Palladian Bridge, Prior Park, Bath, England. 1755

102–3: The Thames, Westminster Bridge (designed by Thomas Page, 1862), and Big Ben, London, England

104: San Giorgio Maggiore and campanile, Venice, Italy

105: The Thames, Blackfriars Bridge (designed by James Cubitt, 1869), and Saint Paul's, London, England

106: The Seine, Pont Neuf (designed by Androuet de Cerceau, 1607), and Île de la Cité, Paris, France

107: Bangkok, Thailand

108–9: Near the Grand Canal, Suzhou, China

110: Kintai Bridge, Iwakuni, Japan. 1673. Reconstructed 1953

111: Bureau of Reclamation. Hoover Dam, Arizona Nevada border. 1931–36

112: Ricardo Legorreta. Solana: a joint venture of Maguire Thomas Partners and IBM, Southlake, Texas. 1986

113: Louis I. Kahn. Salk Institute for Biological Studies, La Jolla, California. 1959–65

114–15: Carlo Scarpa. Brion Cemetery, San Vito d'Altivole, Italy. 1969

116–17: Court of the Lions, The Alhambra, Granada, Spain. Mid-14th century

118–19: John Russell Pope. Jefferson Memorial, Washington, D.C. 1943 (Tidal Basin planned by United States Army Corps of Engineers, completed 1900)

130, 132: Roger Deweese Inc. & Associates (fountain); WZMH Group California, Inc. (building). Wateridge Marketing Pavilion, San Diego, California. Completed 1983

131: Robert Mills, Washington Monument, Washington, D.C. 1848–85

133: Peter Walker. Plaza Tower, Costa Mesa, California. 1991

134: Victor Carrasco. Lap pool, private home built within late medieval fortifications with modern renovations, Bornos, Spain. 1989–90

135: Arquitectonica, Bernardo Fort-Brescia & Laurinda Spear. The Pink House, Miami, Florida. 1978

136–37: Charles W. Moore and William Turnbull with Perez Associates. World's Fair Wonder Wall, New Orleans, Louisiana. 1982–84

138: Court of the Myrtles, The Alhambra, Granada, Spain. Mid-14th century

139, 141: Julia Morgan. Roman Pool (indoor), Hearst Castle, San Simeon, California. 1927–32

140: Julia Morgan. Neptune Pool (outdoor), Hearst Castle, San Simeon, California. 1935–36

142: King's Bath, Bath, England. 12th century

143: Roman Bath and Abbey, Bath, England. 1st century A.D.

144, 146: Claude Monet's water garden, Giverny, France. Begun 1893

145: Henry Hoare. Stourhead Gardens, Wiltshire, England. Begun 1741

147: Shugaku-in, near Kyoto, Japan. Mid-17th century

148–49: Fujiwara Yorimichi. Phoenix Hall, Byodo-in, Kyoto. 1053

150: Zhouzheng Yuan, Suzhou, China. Early 16th century

151: Temple West Garden, Suzhou, China. Begun late 16th century

152: Reflection of Kinkaku-ji, Kyoto, Japan. Gardens begun early 15th century, pavilion rebuilt 1955

153: Peter Muller. Pool, Amandari, Ubud, Bali. 1989

154–55: Yoshio Taniguchi and Shinsuke Takamiya. Tokyo Sea Life Park, Japan. 1987–89

166: Sandcastle, San Francisco, California

167–69: Mont-Saint-Michel, Normandy, France. Begun 1024

170: Tanah Lot, Bali. 15th century

171: Ulu Danu, Lake Bratan, Bali

172: Lopez Island docks, San Juan Islands, Washington

173: Philipsburg, Saint Maarten, Dutch West Indies

174: Lawrence Halprin. Levi Strauss Plaza, San Francisco, California. 1982

175: Ogawa Jihei. Heian Jingu, Kyoto, Japan. 1895

176: Charles W. Moore with the Urban Innovations Group. Oceanside Civic Center, California. 1985

177: Victor Carrasco. Private home built within late medieval fortifications with modern renovations, Bornos, Spain. 1989–90

178–79: Yoshio Taniguchi and Shinsuke Takamiya. Tokyo Sea Life Park, Japan. 1987–89

180: Bassetti, Norton, Metler, and Rekevics, architects; Kramer, Chin, and Mayo, engineers. Seattle Aquarium, Washington. 1977

181: Bill Watts, Enartec, and Marine World Africa U.S.A. "Shark Experience," Marine World Africa U.S.A., Vallejo, California. 1992

182: Maritime Theater, Hadrian's Villa, Tivoli, Italy. A.D.118–25

183: Architectural Services Department. Cultural Center Plaza, Kowloon, Hong Kong. 1989

184: Palazzo Ducale and campanile, Piazza San Marco, Venice, Italy

185: Hong Kong

186: Portofino, Italy

187: Port de Gustavia, Saint Barthélemy, French West Indies

188–89: Moore, Lyndon, Turnbull, Whitaker. Sea Ranch Condominium, Sea Ranch, California. 1963–65

190: Cruise ship, Caribbean

191: Joseph Strauss, engineer; Irving Morrow, architect. Golden Gate Bridge, San Francisco, California. 1937

192–93: Torii Gate, near Miyajima Island, Inland Sea, Japan. Rebuilt 1875

194–95: Isamu Noguchi. "Water Use" Fountain, California Scenario, Costa Mesa, California. 1980–82

196: Frank Lloyd Wright. Fallingwater, Bear Run, Pennsylvania. 1936

205: John Russell Pope. Jefferson Memorial, Washington, D.C. 1943 (Tidal Basin planned by United States Army Corps of Engineers, completed 1900)

206–7: Customs House and Santa Maria della Salute, Venice, Italy

208–9: Howard Fields & Associates. Grand Wailea Resort, Maui, Hawaii. 1991

210: Bang Pa-in, Thailand. Begun 1629, remodeled 1872–89

211: Zhouzheng Yuan, Suzhou, China. Early 16th century

212: Atlandia Design. The Mirage, Las Vegas, Nevada. 1989

213: Roman Bath, Bath, England, 1st century A.D.

214–15: Yoshio Taniguchi and Shinsuke Takamiya. Tokyo Sea Life Park, Japan. 1987–89

INDEX

EDITORS: Harriet Whelchel, Margaret Donovan
DESIGNERS: Dana Sloan, Beth Tondreau
PICTURE RESEARCH: Colin Scott

ILLUSTRATION CREDITS

Architectural renderings on the following pages were made by Kevin Keim: 40, 44–45, 78–85, 122–123, 124 above, 126, 129, 162, 165. Additional illustration credits are: Alinari, Florence: 17, 19, 23; Giraudon: 127 above; U.S. Geodetic Service: 128 below

LIBRARY OF CONGRESS CATALOGING-IN-PUBLICATION DATA

Moore, Charles Willard, 1925–
        Water and architecture / text by Charles W. Moore;
photographs by Jane Lidz.
    p. 224 cm.
        Includes index.
        ISBN 0–8109–3975–4
        1. Water and architecture. I. Lidz, Jane. II. Title.
NA2542.8.M66   1994
720'.47—dc20   93–27389